ADVANCE STUDIES IN LIFELONG EDUCATION

# LIFELONG EDUCATION:
## A Psychological Analysis

# LIFELONG EDUCATION
## A Psychological Analysis

by

## A. J. CROPLEY

*University of Regina, Regina, Saskatchewan, Canada*

*and*

*UNESCO Institute for Education, Hamburg,
Federal Republic of Germany*

LIBRARY
I.M. MARSH COLLEGE OF PHYSICAL EDUCATION
BARKHILL ROAD, LIVERPOOL, 17.

## PERGAMON PRESS
OXFORD · NEW YORK · TORONTO · SYDNEY · PARIS · FRANKFURT

| U.K. | Pergamon Press Ltd., Headington Hill Hall, Oxford OX3 0BW, England |
| U.S.A. | Pergamon Press Inc., Maxwell House, Fairview Park, Elmsford, New York 10523, U.S.A. |
| CANADA | Pergamon of Canada Ltd., 75 The East Mall, Toronto, Ontario, Canada |
| AUSTRALIA | Pergamon Press (Aust.) Pty. Ltd., 19a Boundary Street, Rushcutters Bay, N.S.W. 2011, Australia |
| FRANCE | Pergamon Press SARL, 24 Rue des Ecoles, 75240 Paris, Cedex 05, France |
| FEDERAL REPUBLIC OF GERMANY | Pergamon Press GmbH, 6242 Kronberg-Taunus, Pferdstrasse 1, Federal Republic of Germany |

Copyright © 1977 Unesco Institute of Education

*All Rights Reserved. No part of this publication may be reproduced, stored in a retrieval system or transmitted in any form or by any means: electronic, electrostatic, magnetic tape, mechanical, photocopying, recording or otherwise, without permission in writing from the copyright holders*

First edition 1977
Reprinted 1978

**Library of Congress Cataloging in Publication Data**

Cropley, A. J.
Lifelong education.

(Advances in lifelong education; v. 3)
Bibliography: p.
Includes index.
1. Adult education. I. Title. II. Series.
LC5219.C74        374        77-5702
ISBN 0-08-021814-8( Hardcover )    374  CRO  HOI  pre
ISBN 0-08-021815-6( Flexicover )

*In order to make this volume available as economically and rapidly as possible the author's typescript has been reproduced in its original form. This method unfortunately has its typographical limitations but it is hoped that they in no way distract the reader.*

"The UNESCO Institute for Education, Hamburg, is a legally independent entity. While the programmes of the Institute are established along the lines laid down by the General Conference of UNESCO, the publications of the Institute are issued under its sole responsibility; UNESCO is not responsible for their content.

The points of view, selection of facts and opinions expressed are those of the author and do not necessarily coincide with official positions of the UNESCO Institute for Education, Hamburg."

*Printed in Great Britain by Page Bros (Norwich) Ltd, Norwich*

# Contents

# Foreword

Quantitative and qualitative developments taking place in education in both developed and developing countries in recent years, together with increasing constraints such as shortage of funds, are resulting in the search for ways of organizing educational services so that they will be more democratic, more flexible, better adapted to the needs and requirements of society, and more responsive to the perceived problems and dangers of contemporary life.

The International Commission for the Development of Education and Unesco have recently proposed lifelong education as a master concept for the organization of education at all levels and in all kinds of societies. In response to the call for clarification and practical implementation of this guiding concept, the Unesco Institute for Education decided, in May 1972, to focus its international, cooperative research programme on school level education within the perspective of lifelong learning.

The present volume represents one step in this process of theoretical elucidation and practical specification of the concept of lifelong education. It involves an analysis of some of the major theoretical assumptions of lifelong education, through consideration of its psychological basis. It also attempts to indicate, although in broad and general terms, some of the main features of school curriculum from the point of view of lifelong education.

The present text has been prepared with a wide audience in mind. It should provide a useful introduction to the basic ideas underlying "lifelong education" for those who are newcomers to the area. It should also help scholars to focus their thinking on certain key issues, and to examine some of the statements made in this connection with more penetrating critical thought. It will also hopefully be valuable to instructors

in teacher training institutions, and to students preparing to
enter the teaching professsion, both as an introduction to the
basic notions of lifelong education, and also as a review of
educational psychology relevant to the area.
    The Unesco Institute for Education has been fortunate in
benefiting from the cooperation of Professor Arthur Cropley,
who has been associated with the current programme of the Institute since it first began in 1973, for the preparation of
this study.  Grateful acknowledgement must also be made of
those contributions from friends and staff members of the Institute to the preparation of the final version of this study.


                              M. Dino Carelli

                              Director
                              Unesco Institute for Education

# Introduction

The set of educational goals and ideals referred to as involving "lifelong education" is increasingly being referred to
in contemporary educational theory, after first appearing in
ancient writings and subsequently re-emerging from time to time
throughout the middle ages and relatively modern times. It has
even been proposed as the master concept for the development of
present day world education in both developed and developing
nations. However, the principles set down as guidelines for future educational developments have often been couched in idealistic terms or have made many assumptions about factors such as
what might loosely be called "human nature", or about other crucial preconditions such as the economic feasibility of a lifelong system of education. For these reasons, there is a pressing need for more precise definition of just what is meant by
lifelong education. It is also important to show what novelty
the principle contains, and in what way it is of particular relevance to contemporary educational issues. Finally, there is
need of statements concerning the practical implications of the
ideals of lifelong education for teachers in the classroom, for
those who are concerned with training teachers, for educational
planners, and for all other elements of the educational system.

It would be excessively ambitious to attempt to meet all
of these needs in a single volume, and certainly no such attempt has been made here. However, what has been attempted is
a contribution in the area. The present book adopts the standpoint of psychology, and examines some of the relevant issues
from this standpoint. It is concerned with teasing out some of
the key issues and problems, and trying to show what kind of
factors need to be borne in mind when evaluating lifelong education or attempting to apply its principles. It is also concerned with the question of whether the basic assumptions underlying lifelong education make good sense, psychologically speak-

9

ing.  Finally, it is concerned with what school curriculum
would be like, in very general terms, if lifelong education
were adopted as a guiding principle for its design.  This analysis of curriculum is necessarily general and abstract, but it
is hoped that it represents a move in the direction of giving
practical application to the prescriptions put forward in the
name of lifelong education.

The text deals at some length with criticisms of lifelong
education.  Indeed, it may even seem that many of the criticisms are endorsed, or that they are advanced with excessive
enthusiasm.  However, this approach is adopted because review
of criticism and self-evalution as a result is one of the major forms of learning.  From criticism comes improvement; for
this reason careful consideration of critical comments should
be one of the activities of proponents of lifelong education.
The book is also limited in several ways.  For example, it reflects the author's own judgment concerning the most useful
psychological authorities to consult and, for this reason, it
will be judged inadequate or defective by some readers.  It is
certainly selective and incomplete.  This seems to be inevitable and unavoidable unless an attempt is made to be encyclo-
paedic in coverage.  The book also neglects writings in languages other than English, French and German, something which
reflects the author's linguistic inadequacies and not a judgment of quality.

The major work involved in the writing of this book was
done at the Unesco Institute for Education.  However, its preparation was greatly facilitated by several months spent as a
Visiting Professor in the Psychology Department at the University of Adelaide.  I am very grateful to the Department there
for its assistance.  I am also grateful to the University of
Regina, where I have an appointment as Professor of Psychology,
for making leave available to me so that I could continue my
studies in the area of lifelong education.  The greatest debt,
however, is owed to my friends and colleagues at the Unesco Institute.  Ursula Giere has been invaluable in her help from the
Documentation Centre, Louise Silz has made my work much easier
as a result of her loyal and skilful secretarial assistance,
and Louise Ortmann has made the task of physical production of
the text a much lighter load.  Johanna Kesavan made an important contribution through her critical editing of the manuscript, and her suggestions have led to the elimination of many
faults.  Many others, too, have helped generously and cheer-
fully.  I have had much help from visitors to the Institute,
and especially from our colleagues who have worked with us on
a number of research projects in the area of lifelong education,

and from those who were kind enough to read and criticize the manuscript. I think in particular of Rod Skager, Ettore Gelpi, Paul Lengrand, and many others. I am also grateful to Peter Sachsenmeier for his help in bringing me into contact with Pergamon Press. However, the most crucial factors were the provision by Dr. M.D. Carelli, in his capacity as Director of the Unesco Institute for Education, of the freedom to read, think and write, and above all, the influence of my colleague and mentor Dr. R.H. Dave, who shaped much of my thinking in the area.

A.J. Cropley

# Chapter 1

# Modern Education and the Challenge of Change

*Education for coping with change*

Many educators are becoming increasingly concerned by the rapid changes taking place in almost all spheres of modern life. In the socio-cultural domain, for example, there has been enormous population growth, greatly increased social mobility, and wider public participation in political and cultural activities. One effect of these kinds of change has been increasing demand for educational equality, both within societies and also between nations of differing wealth and technological development. Changes have also been seen in communications, in science, and in technology. Finally, there have been extensive changes in the availability of and demand for consumer goods, and in the organization of the means of their production. As a result, in the vocational world some jobs are disappearing, while new ones are emerging which require new kinds of skill. Because of these phenomena, today's schoolchildren may be preparing to enter a social and vocational world that will not exist at the time they become adults. This is true of both highly-developed countries and also of less-developed.

Educational innovators are thus beginning to emphasize the need for a new educational goal -- education for a changing world. This goal is one that has profound implications of a psychological nature. It also has implications for many other aspects of human life, but it is the psychological ones with which the present volume will be mainly concerned. The new goal (education for coping with change) suggests that skills, values and attitudes which children are spending their childhoods acquiring, in areas such as knowledge-getting, interpersonal relations, self-development, and sense of individuality, may no longer be relevant to the world they will live in as adults.

For example, an increasing need is seen for "innovative knowledge" (Dumazedier, 1972), in which present knowledge will serve as the basis for a continuous process of further learning and re-learning. This process of continuous learning will not be restricted to the traditional three Rs of school, but will be extended to all psychological domains. Children will need to acquire knowledge not only of the facts and processes of their society's technological and social organization, but of themselves, of other people, and of their own and other cultures. In the domain of traditional learning they will need to know how to locate knowledge as and when they want it, but even more importantly, how to use knowledge. They will have to be able to organize, store and recall information, to handle logical and numerical operations, and to communicate with other people.

In recent educational theory, emphasis is also moving away from education's role in the provision of cognitive skills and focussing more on that of fostering interpersonal and intrapersonal development. There are increasing demands that education consciously strive to facilitate full and satisfactory personal growth and increased self-actualization. It should develop individuals who, as part of the process of growth towards maturity, become psychologically equipped to cope with the personal tensions resulting from rapid economic, vocational, social and cultural change. Many children who would, for instance, have entered agricultural occupations 20 years ago will have to be enabled by their schooling, not only to acquire technological, urban-oriented job skills, but also to derive personally satisfying lives from this kind of work. Increasing urbanization has thus eroded traditional work values. It has also changed parent-child, male-female, and worker-boss relationships, as a result of factors like expanding automation of industry, widespread availability of cheap power, massive reduction in the need for unskilled labour, and disappearance of the small, hand-worked farm.

Changes of the kinds just discussed have implications going beyond their effects on the production and distribution of goods and the achievement of job security, however. Indeed, it is predicted that widespread change will produce a future world of personal and emotional instability. If people cannot cope with change, they will be exposed to the risk of submergence, overwhelming or alienation of their individualities. In such a climate education will have to take on the roles of fostering the growth of strong personalities capable of coping with change, and of helping people to relate to other people. In short, in addition to its responsibilities in the cognitive

domain, education must help students develop new concepts of
self development, and of independence, to be applied to understanding oneself, to relationships with other people, to work
and to leisure.


*Educational needs of adults*

Another criticism of contemporary educational systems is
that they do not adequately provide for the needs of the largest
single segment of society -- adults. It is argued that whereas
children will have to deal with the changes of the future at
some later time when they grow up, those who are already adults
have no such period of grace. They are already embroiled in
the momentous changes of the present. Thus, there is increasing
emphasis on the view that while education should certainly be
concerned with equipping the children of the present to cope
with the changes of the future, educational systems should also
be organized in such a way as to be capable of meeting the present needs of those who are already adult. The assumption that
10, 12 or 15 years of formal schooling at some time in the past
have equipped adults to cope with their entire lives is losing
favour in current educational thinking. Some signs of this increasing concern with the education of adults are, for example,
the growth of Adult Education in North America, and the development of organizational principles such as that of "recurrent
education". Recently enacted legislation in France required
employers to set aside substantial sums for the further education of their employees, some German states have established
periods of *Bildungsurlaub* (educational leave), while some Australian trade unions and employers have recently agreed upon
contracts providing paid leave for employees to attend educational courses. The success of the Open University in Britain,
and steps to develop similar institutions in some other countries, schemes like the decentralized teaching of practising
Social Workers in Canada, and similar developments, are examples of the burgeoning interest in the education of adults.
There is, then, a felt need in a world of change for provision
of formal educative experiences to people beyond the conventional school years.


*Education and early childhood*

A third strand of argument concerns the importance of experience in the earliest years of life in shaping future development. Although, in some cases, their claims may have been

based more on economic or political issues than on an analysis
of the psychology of early childhood, many groups in highly-
developed countries have, in recent years, been subjecting gov-
ernments to increasing pressure to make formal provision for
the education of very young children. This has often been
couched in terms of pre-school care for the children of working
mothers. In some societies (e.g., Canada) early childhood education has also been proposed as a device for facilitating the
eventual amalgamation of children of ethnic minority groups
(such as Canadian Indians) into the dominant culture. Widespread attention has also been paid in educational circles to
projects involving early education such as the "Headstart" program in the U.S.A., aimed at remedying cognitive defects suf-
fered as a result of inadequate early stimulation. Certainly,
the importance of experience in the earliest years of life is
now widely recognized. One result is a call for some degree of
formal structuring of the learning experiences of pre-school
children (i.e., for schooling to be extended downwards from
today's age limits). Again, then, there is a felt need for an
expanded concept of schooling.

*Genuine educational equality*

    A separate broad line of attack on conventional education-
al organization that is relevant at this point arises from the
changing conceptualization of educational equality that has
emerged in recent writings. Equality was initially seen as a
matter of providing physical facilities of equal standard to
all schoolchildren, regardless of socio-economic status, race,
and similar factors. Recent reports in the U.S.A., however,
have suggested that equality in this sense is closer to being
realized in that country than had previously been thought.
Nevertheless, despite this, inequities in time spent at school,
possession of school skills, rates of entry to prestigeous occupations, and so on, still exist. Consequently, it is being
argued that educational reforms are needed which will go far
beyond "patching up" the existing system. True educational
equality will only exist when all people in a society profit
equally from educational facilities, even if, for reasons such
as lack of interest in schooling during childhood, they do not
utilize the educational opportunities available to them during
conventional school years. There is, in fact, strong pressure
for the development of systems of education which promote actual *equality of end result*, and not merely *equality of theoretical access to facilities*, both between the various social

strata within given societies, and also across societies of
differing wealth and technological development.

## Lifelong education

Thus, educational thinking in recent years has stressed
that the current organization of schooling does not take adequate account of the fact that we live in a changing world. Adjusting in such a way as to counter this criticism is the challenge education now faces.

About ten years ago, various agencies of UNESCO began to
examine systematically the implications for educational organization of the kinds of criticisms just mentioned. Their deliberations have led to the description of an educational principle which, it is now claimed, should be accepted as the basis
of the whole organization of education -- the principle of lifelong education. The basic notion is that education should be
formally conceptualized as a process which continues throughout
an individual's life, from earliest childhood to old age. Of
course, widespread informal recognition already exists that education, in the sense of profiting from experience, does go on
throughout life. What is advocated here is that this knowledge
should be systematized and incorporated into the design of
schooling. Furthermore, this lifelong process is seen as highly integrated and interactive, with events at one age level
being both partly determined by those at earlier ages, and also
partly determining those in the future. This is the principle
of "vertical integration". Moreover, the relationship between
education and life is seen as being so close as to require integration of education with the other major aspects of life,
such as home, work, leisure, social life, and so on. This is
the principle of "horizontal integration". (These basic concepts of lifelong education will be examined in more detail in
Chapter 2.)

## The role of psychology

The commitment of UNESCO to the principle of lifelong education means that a major international educational body has
adopted lifelong education. Consequently, it is appropriate
that the concept should be examined in a systematic and organized manner, and the present text is an attempt to carry out
one such examination -- from the point of view of psychology.
Like any theory of educational organization, lifelong education
has a psychological base. Of course, it also has bases in dis-

ciplines other than psychology, and its acceptance or rejection
will also depend upon these bases. However, the present text
is mainly restricted to a psychological analysis. This analysis has five main aspects, which are the following:

1. Presentation of the main psychological features
   of descriptions of lifelong education.
2. Statement of the main arguments for lifelong education in psychological terms.
3. Review of the evidence for the validity of these
   arguments.
4. Analysis of the implications of psychological
   knowledge for school curriculum if it were to
   be re-organized within a lifelong education
   framework.
5. Examination of the criticisms of lifelong education that have recently been advanced, and specification of some of their implications for further
   study of lifelong education.

The review of psychological material is, of course, highly
selective. In this respect it obviously involves judgments
concerning the most pertinent and informative writings in the
area, and as a result, much material which another person might
well have included has been omitted. In addition to this more
or less idiosyncratic basis and the effects of familiarity or
lack of familiarity with various writers' work, two other principles were loosely applied in the selection of material. The
first of these was that, except where a deliberate attempt was
made to review early theory and research for the purpose of
contrasting older with more recent points of view, there was
concentration on the work of contemporary writers, or at least
on the work of writers who were still active up to about 10
years ago. The second informal rule was that there was heavy
emphasis on conclusions and generalizations derived from empirical studies conforming at least loosely to the "scientific"
method. This approach was not followed rigidly, and served
merely as a rough guideline for selection of material. However,
it resulted in only passing reference to some writers such as
Freud, and heavy emphasis on the conclusions of others such as
Hunt.
A second major exclusion results from concentration on
writings in English, French and German. Because of this "language barrier", there is no doubt that some relevant research
in other languages has been overlooked. The notion of lifelong
education has aroused widespread interest, so that other researchers with greater knowledge of languages would undoubtedly

be in a position to add to the analysis made here, for example
through reference to important writing in Arabic, Chinese and
the Slav languages.  In any case, it is necessary to acknowledge that the present volume is limited to only portion of the
scholarship in the area, and to remind readers that a wider
literature is available.  It has been omitted here only because
of the present author's personal limitations, and not because
it has been judged to be of lesser interest.


*Structure of the present text*

Two broad tasks have just been outlined.  They involve examination of lifelong education's psychological assumptions on
the one hand, and indication of psychology's implications for a
lifelong education-oriented system on the other.  Both are attempted in the present text.  The second chapter involves a
more detailed analysis of the arguments advanced to support the
concept of lifelong education.  Chapter 3 shows how psychological knowledge can, and indeed should, be applied to the analysis of lifelong education in order to test whether the principle has any legitimacy.  Chapters 4, 5 and 6 review findings
concerning psychological functioning throughout life, in order
to test whether the principles of lifelong education are indeed
based upon reasonable conclusions about the nature of psychological functioning over a wide range of ages.  Chapter 7 spells
out the implications of earlier sections of the text for schooling as we currently know it, and indicates how schooling might
be modified in order to enable it to serve the goals of lifelong education.  Finally, Chapter 8 contains a critical evaluation of lifelong education, with emphasis on the psychological
issues, but including a somewhat more wide-ranging critique.
The purpose of this chapter is to strengthen and improve understanding of lifelong education, not to condemn it.  The overall
aim of the book is to define the key features of the principle
of lifelong education, to demonstrate that the basic line of
argument makes a certain degree of sense in the light of current psychological knowledge, and to indicate what formal
schooling might be like if the principle were adopted (if
schools as we know them survived in a system which was so committed).

# Chapter 2

# Basic Concepts in Lifelong Education

## WHAT IS LIFELONG EDUCATION?

The 1972 report of the International Commission on the Development of Education, published by UNESCO and now referred to as the "Faure Report" (Faure, 1972), contained as its very first recommendation for educational planners the proposal that so-called "lifelong education" should be adopted as the "master concept" for future educational innovation. This was recommended for both developed and developing countries (Faure, 1972, p. 182). Since then, the idea has received considerable attention and has become widely known. However, examination of the literature (e.g. Dave, 1973) suggests that, even in Europe, it is not fully understood, and that complete consensus concerning its nature, rationale, and educational implications does not exist. Furthermore, it seems to be much less well-known in educational circles outside Europe. Consequently, the present chapter contains an introductory summary of some of the main principles of lifelong education as they are described in the relevant literature. The purpose of these sections is not to review the literature in great detail. This has already been done in publications such as that of Dave (1973). What is intended here is to give an idea of basic thinking in the area, and to establish the meaning of the term "lifelong education" as it is used in the present text.

### Difference from adult education

To some extent, the label "lifelong education" is self-explanatory. However, it is important to distinguish it from, for example, the more traditional process of adult education. A great deal more is implied by the notion of lifelong education than extension of adult education to a wider audience, or

19

the provision of more upgrading classes for workers who are
barred from further advancement in their jobs by inadequate
skills.  The mere existence of even well developed adult education facilities does not mean that lifelong education has been
achieved (Farmer, 1974).  For example, there is the problem
that adult education is highly selective, largely as a result
of the "second creaming" (Bengtsson, 1975, p. 9) - those who
already have the most education tend to seek adult education,
rather than those who presumably need it most.  Furthermore
adult education is not presently organized as something which
is closely integrated with and co-ordinated to earlier education.  At the moment adult education is still conceptualized as
either recreation or else something which ought to be under-
taken by those who need to compensate for earlier shortcomings.
Thus it is stigmatized as being either a luxury or else remedial
rather than being regarded as a normal part of an ongoing process of education throughout life.  For example, the argument
that people go to school largely in order to prepare themselves
for later adult education would probably seem absurd, even to
most adult educators.  These remarks are not intended to dis-
parage adult education as it currently exists, nor to imply
that the under-qualified worker would not be provided for in
an educational system organized along the lines of lifelong education.  However, the purposes of lifelong education are considerably broader than vocational upgrading or the increasing
of workers' productivity (as indeed are those of adult education).  A lifelong education-oriented system would, in fact,
subsume adult education as it currently exists, while simultaneously breaking down the distinction between adult education and
any other kind of education.  This point will become more apparent later in the present chapter.


*Traditional role of school*

     School has traditionally been regarded as confined to a
specific age-group (usually from about 6 to about 18), although
it is now being recognized that there is no evidence that learning is really most efficient or desirable between these ages
(Coste, 1973, p. 47; Rohwer, 1971).  Furthermore, school has
traditionally been concerned with information rather than with
education in the moral, ethical or socio-affective domains (e.g.
Coleman, 1972).  Even where information is concerned, the emphasis has been on mastering bodies of facts, not on acquiring
skill in learning.  As Silva (1973, p. 41) put it, the student
has been conceptualized as "a mere receptacle or 'stockpot' of

knowledge." The information transmitted is seen as a summary
of the basic things the student will need to know in later life.
This knowledge is not usually expressly designed to be relevant
to the immediate, day-to-day life of students (although such
immediate practical application may occur as a lucky "acci-
dent"). Its usefulness lies in the adult life to come. Finally, school has been traditionally conceived of as preparing
students to play well-defined roles in an existing social structure (e.g., Bowles, 1971), and as imparting a set of vocational
skills which are linked to those social roles and are necessary
for vocational success during adult life (e.g., Kyöstiö, 1972).
One of the effects of this traditional conceptualization of the
role of school has been not only to divorce schooling from the
day-to-day real lives of students, but to dissociate learning
in school, from other sources of knowledge such as libraries,
museums, the home, work, social organizations, and so on.

*Lifelong education*

The basic philosophy of lifelong education expressly questions the traditional conceptualization of school that has just
been described. As Dave (1973, pp, 11-12) has emphasized, physiological growth, personality development, and social, economic
and cultural growth all continue throughout life. Lifelong education rests on the belief that learning too occurs throughout
life, albeit in different ways and through differing processes.
The latter point has been extensively discussed in the works of
developmental psychologists such as Bruner (see Bruner and Olson, 1973, for a recent discussion). According to Stephens
(1967), both learning and teaching are natural events in which
the human species continually engages in a spontaneous manner,
even without necessarily being aware of doing it. Thus, it is
argued that learning should be supported and fostered from the
earliest years to old age. The key notion in lifelong education is that all individuals ought to have organized and systematic opportunities for instruction, study and learning at
any time throughout their lives. This is true whether their
goals are to remedy earlier educational defects, to acquire new
skills, to upgrade themselves vocationally, to increase their
understanding of the world in which they live, to develop their
own personalities, or some other purposes. In this framework,
education is basically seen as serving to facilitate personal
development throughout life, in the broadest sense of the term
"development" (e.g. Lengrand, 1970, p. 46). Lifelong education
is regarded as an organizing principle which will ultimately

make it possible for education to serve this function. It is
" 'a process of change' leading to the development of the individual " (Silva, 1973, p. 41).

Such a model of education is, of course, not entirely novel. The conceptualization of education as a tool for developing individuals who will learn throughout life and thus become
more valuable to society is to be found in the writings of both
Matthew Arnold (see for example Johnson, 1972), and Comenius
(see Kyrasek & Polisensky, 1968), as well as educational writers in antiquity. Dewey (1916, pp. 90-91) expressed the view
that education and learning are lifelong processes over 60 years
ago. A report to the British Government at the end of the first
world war (Ministry of Reconstruction Adult Education Committee,
1919) specifically recommended that education should be "lifelong", as a matter of national importance. However, it is apparent that in the 60 years or more since Dewey's recommendations for the U.S. and the Ministry of Reconstruction's recommendations for the U.K., truly lifelong-oriented educational
systems have not been developed.

## WHY LIFELONG EDUCATION?

Proponents of lifelong education advance in its favour a
number of arguments of different kinds. It is argued that it
will increase equity in the distribution of educational services, that it has favourable economic implications, that it is
essential in the face of a changing social structure, that there
are strong vocational reasons for establishing it, that it will
lead to an improved quality of life, and so on.

### Equity

As Lengrand (1970, pp. 26-27), for example, has shown,
there are powerful social forces at work today which urge that
all societies and all strata of each society should have full
opportunity to realize their own potentials, and that they
should have equal access to social, economic and political advantages. Pressures for equality of educational opportunity
are not new, but they are being applied with renewed vigour in
highly developed societies such as the U.S.A. (e.g., Coleman,
1966; Jencks, 1972). Furthermore, they are also being felt in
developing countries, where it is argued that retention of traditional educational systems inherited from former colonial powers will inhibit national development to levels of international equality (e.g., Hinzen and Hundsdörfer, 1977; Parkyn, 1973).

Despite widespread desire for equality both within and between nations, many observers contend that school as it presently exists serves essentially to preserve the status quo (e.g. Ward, 1972, pp. 179-181), since students are trained to fit a certain social niche and so to perpetuate the existing order. According to this argument, knowledge is treated in traditional schools as primarily a commodity to be consumed (e.g., Weaver, 1972, pp. 171), and inequality is maintained by the controlling influence of an educational establishment with a vested interest in keeping knowledge in short supply. This kind of argument is summarized by Bowles's statement (1971, p. 178) that school serves primarily for "the reproduction of the social relations of production". By contrast, lifelong education is said to be a principle which would eliminate this role of the school as an instrument for perpetuating inequity.

*Economic considerations*

The cost of education is apparently approaching the point at which society can no longer bear it. For developing countries this problem is particularly acute, as the example of Upper Volta demonstrates (see Elvin, 1975). This nation spends about 18% of its revenues on education and yet the enormous expenditure, relative to the government's total income, provides education to only about 10% of the country's school age population. Provision of education to 100% would apparently require expenditures equivalent to 1.8 times the entire national budget. Even in technologically advanced nations, some school systems are threatened with bankruptcy (Coste, 1973, p. 46). At the same time, there is increasing demand for greater and greater educational services, wider accessibility of schooling, and more diverse kinds of education. Expedients which have been suggested for meeting the financial crisis have included performance contracting, introduction of voucher systems, increasing use of educational technology, and so on (e.g., Cropley & Gross, 1973).

However, all efforts, including the expenditure of higher proportions of the world's gross national products, have failed to bring universal literacy nearer in developing nations, to eliminate illiteracy in the developed ones, or to meet the educational needs of all sectors of all societies. For example, although the number of children in the world attending school rose between 1960 and 1968 from 325 to 460 million, the number of school-age children to whom educational services were not available increased by 17 million in the same period (Faure, 1972). Much the same can be said for adults. According to

Elvin (1975), there has recently been an increase of over 80
million in the number of adult illiterates (the exact increase
depending upon the definition of illiteracy employed).  This
sad state of affairs is even more disappointing when it is set
in an economic context.  During the very period when the number
of children not able to attend school was increasing, the proportion of the world's GNP's that was being spend on education
rose from 3.02% to 4.24% (Faure, 1972), an increase that reflects very great effort on the part of developing nations in
particular.

     Thus, the question arises of whether any of the expedients
that have been proposed have the potential to cope with the economic issues currently facing educational systems.  In the
main, such alternative strategies have really been nothing but
modified ways of delivering and/or financing the same product --
a traditional education.  Unlike such expedients, lifelong education involves a radically new model of the educational process.  As such, it is clear that it would have profound economic
implications.  Nonetheless, Coste (1973, p. 48) has sounded a
warning by concluding that modifying the ages at which formal
schooling takes place is unlikely to yield monetary savings in
the cost of education.  Indeed, it is difficult to remember any
educational "reform" which has not led to *increased* costs!

     One economic case for adopting a system of lifelong educa-
tion has been stated by Zhamin and Kostanian (1972).  Although
admitting that it is very difficult to calculate the cash return to a nation from increased educational expenditure, they
give actual statistical example of the better work performance
of more highly-educated workers, and estimate that between 1960
and 1968 the "economic return" to the Soviet Union of one extra
rouble spent on education was an increase of four roubles in
the Gross National Product.  Thus, they see the establishment
of an educational system which functions as "the basis for acquisition of skills of a new type" as economically rewarding
for a society.  It is important to re-emphasize here that most
proponents of lifelong education do not advocate its adoption
simply to increase workers' productivity, and thus increase
profits.  Indeed, this approach has specifically been rejected
by writers such as Vinokur (1976).  Of much greater importance
are questions like improved quality of life, greater self-fulfilment, or liberation from ignorance, poverty or exploitation.
Nonetheless, there is increasingly clear recognition, expecial-
ly in developing nations, that education serves as the basis
for a modern economy.  Furthermore, such an economy leads to a
higher standard of living, with all the benefits of increased
life expectancy, better physical health, greater happiness, and

the like. (See the chapters by Nyerere in Hinzen and Hundsdörfer, 1977, for a clear review of this connection, and of the
demands it places upon education.) Recognition of a relationship between education and economic development and of the subsequent improvement of personal and social life, thus provides
a further economic argument for a radical change in the organization of education, since education, economic development
and improved quality of life are intimately connected.

*Social factors -- the changing role of the family*

According to Coleman (1972, p. 431), the family functioned
as a major source of education in the past. However, he argues
that this situation has now changed markedly, so that it has
come to play a lesser and lesser role in children's education.
This is especially noticeable in the areas of moral, affective
and social education. A further eroding of the role of the
family may be anticipated as a result of increasing technological growth, increasing urbanization, and increasing complexity of life (Aujaleu, 1973). The consequence Aujaleu foresees
resulting from this reduction in the influence of one of the
most important factors in children's development is a "collapse
of values" (p. 25). This change in the structure of society
and in the role of one of its major institutions (the family)
implies a changed role for education. Specifically, it will
have to find a way of "filling the gap" left by the family.
Lifelong education may conceivably provide an organizational
framework which will permit education to carry out this task.
It should be noted, at this point, that emphasis on the role of
lifelong education as an adjunct to the family implies that it
would expand education to cover the earlier as well as the
later years of life. Hopefully, recognition of the importance
of moral and social education, and emphasis in schools on the
educative role of the family, would also lead to a strengthening
and revitalizing of the influence of the home, in a process of
interaction between the powerful influences.

*Social factors -- changing social roles*

A second set of social changes which is distinct from that
of the changing role of the family although closely related to
it in some ways, includes the changing role of the adolescent
in contemporary society (Hicter, 1972), the changing relationship of the worker to his work and to his bosses, increasing
participation by the citizenry in the political life of commu-

nities, greatly increased leisure, and so on.  In relatively
undeveloped societies, the line between childhood and adulthood has traditionally been very clear.  Admission to the adult
world has frequently involved a specific age and even some kind
of formal initiation ceremony.  The development of complex,
technologically advanced societies, however, has made it necessary for childhood to be extended.  Initially, school may have
provided the major distinction between children and adults
(children go to school, adults work).  However, even this distinction is becoming blurred.  Youthful marriage is increasingly common, more and more former adult privileges are being extended to children, while increasing numbers of adults are re-
turning to school.  Some 18-year-olds may be married and working, while some 30-year-olds are still students.  Childhood,
when traditionally one should be at school, and adulthood, when
one should not, are difficult to separate, so that education is
naturally being extended to a wider and wider age range.
     In a somewhat similar way, the precise social relation-
ships among workers are becoming unclear.  Workers in the future may have to adopt altered social roles which would be deemed today to be more appropriate to bosses.  Other social roles
are altering too, for example in the area of sex stereotyping.
Increasing numbers of women are achieving social positions
which have tended in the past to be closed to them (e.g., bosses, ministers of state, priests, and similar roles).  Allied
to these changes is the changing conception of the male as the
breadwinner.  Thus, decreasing importance of the family, increasing sexual emancipation, uncertainty concerning the status
of children and adolescents, and similar factors all suggest
that education in its present form is poorly organized to help
today's children cope with the social organization that may
exist when they grow up.  As a result, it ought to contain a
strong element of training in playing a wide variety of social
roles (Coles, 1972, p. 178), to make it easier for individuals
to adapt to shifts in their relationship to other people.


*Technological change*

     Closely involved in the kinds of changes just discussed,
and frequently cited by proponents of lifelong education as a
major argument in its favour, is the phenomenon of accelerating
technological change (e.g., Agoston, 1975; Batyshev, 1972;
Hicter, 1972, p. 301; Lengrand, 1970, pp. 15-16).  Technological growth leads to greatly increased availability of information, changing nature of work, increasing urbanization, and

increased leisure (e.g., Worth, 1972), medical benefits such as
lengthening of life and lower infant mortality (Aujaleu, 1973,
p. 23), and greater availability of material possessions, with
the consequent encouragement of worldliness and materialism at
the expense of spiritual and cultural values (Suchodolski,
1976), and the estrangement and alienation of people from each
other (De'Ath, 1976). Thus, it contributes to the growing uncertainty concerning the nature of the vocational world of the
future and also to the erosion of the family, and the uncertainty about social roles and interpersonal relations in the
future. Consequently, it is a significant and ubiquitous factor in the call for a new organizational basis for education.

*Vocational factors*

A point of view met again and again in the literature on
education for the latter portion of the present century is that
the vocational world of the future is likely to be drastically
different from that of today. In this context, the capacity of
educational systems as they are currently organized to provide
children with the specific skills they will need to achieve vocational success in the future is extremely doubtful. Indeed,
there are grounds for suspecting that one of the features of
vocational life of the future may be the occurrence of shifts
in "saleable" vocational skills, not only across generations
(as is presently the case), but within the lifetime of a single
generation. This means that workers of the future may find it
necessary to abandon earlier skills which have served them for
a time, and acquire new ones, possibly several times during the
course of their vocational lifetimes. As has been pointed out,
this shift may also involve changes in inter-relationships with
fellow workers, employers, and so on, so that its effects would
be complex and pervasive.

According to some writers (see Worth, 1972, for a recent
discussion), not only may the relationships of workers to other
people alter, but so too may their relationship to work. Medicine, for example, may become a highly technological activity
(Aujaleu, 1973), requiring new kinds of skills. A whole new
conceptualization of what constitutes work, and of who should
or even may work, may emerge. Increasing penetration of the
work world by automated systems suggests that the nature of
work itself may change. This could involve not only the need
for new kinds of skill, but also a drastic change in the idea
of what kinds of activity constitute working. In highly developed countries, for instance, decreasing importance is now

being attached to work as a means of physical survival. This
is accompanied by increased tolerance of high unemployment in
some countries, as a necessary adjunct to an efficient work economy and reduced levels of inflation.  Some societies have already downgraded work even to the point of providing guaranteed
annual incomes, such as are now seen in some parts of Canada,
regardless of whether recipients work or not.

Thus, in the future, work may serve a function different
from that of providing income, and hence necessities and luxu-
ries (which is still its predominant one today).  It may, for
example, become a means of self-expression, a way of expressing
aggression, a kind of social obligation on a par with participation in parent-teacher groups or rolling bandages for the Red
Cross today, a way of giving public evidence of uprightness or
righteousness, or even conceivably a punishment or a sign of
social inadequacy.  The right to work may even become a sought-
after privilege.  Although these suggestions are probably fan-
ciful, society may see a great change in the social significance of work, the role of work in the life of the individual,
the value placed upon working by both individual and society,
and even the necessity to work.  All of these possibilities suggest that today's children may need for their future lives something quite different from simply a set of pre-packaged vocational skills.   Rather, it seems that education should equip
students with the capacity to react positively to change, both
in terms of continuing capacity to play a vocationally useful
role in society, and also in terms of the ability to maintain
their identities in the face of what may be a very different
kind of work world.

*Needs of adults*

Those who are presently adults are already experiencing
the effects of rapid change in their vocational lives.  For
example, the threat of redundancy or of obsolescence is looming
over many workers.  Furthermore, the obsolescence of skills currently possessed, and the need for the acquisition of new
skills, is by no means confined to workers at the blue collar
levels.   Dubin (1974) has shown that professional engineers are
already struggling with a problem of skill-obsolescence.  According to him, the "half-life" of an average engineering class
taught in an American university is falling continually, and is
now astonishingly short.  The result is that today's practising
engineers in the U.S.A. face the prospect of possessing obsolete knowledge long before their active professional life is

over.  In the future, their skills may be obsolescent within
perhaps five years of completing their degree programmes.  Thus,
for today's adults, the problem of rapidly changing vocational
skills is not merely an abstract problem of the future, but one
which must be faced in the present.

One response to this problem has been a proliferation of
classes for the already-adult in many countries.  However, in
the U.S.A., for example, programmes for the re-training of workers who have become obsolete as a result of changes in the in-
dustries in which they had been employed have often yielded
disappointing results.  One factor has been the unwillingness
of those who need it most to accept new learning, the greatest
interest in further learning being shown by those who are already the best educated (Bengtsson, 1975).  Displaced workers
have expressed feelings of foolishness at having to go back to
school, have rejected re-training as beneath their adult dig-
nity, and so on.  In fact, then, their values and attitudes
have militated against willingness to engage in the new learning which is argued here to be a necessity in today's world.
This problem arises from endorsement of the traditional conceptualization of schooling that has been described in earlier
sections of the present chapter.  An educational system organized in such a way as to foster learning in adulthood throughout all levels of society would therefore, have to break down
the notion that one learns only during formal schooling between
the ages of about 6 and 18.  Thus, it implies radically-changed
views of when one may be schooled and what schooling is.  It
requires, to paraphrase Gelpi (1976), a "politics" of lifelong
education.

## Needs of young children

A second age-group outside the years during which schooling
is normally available is that of young children. As with adults,
recent years have been marked by increasing interest in the
needs of children under six.  In particular, there has been
growing recognition that the early years constitute a stage of
development in their own right, and are not merely a waiting
period prior to childhood, adolescence and adulthood.  It is
now known that infants are much more "competent" than had been
previously been thought (see Stone, Murphy & Smith, 1972, for
example, for an extensive review of the competence of infants
and very young children).  Certainly, small children have considerable capacity for reasoning and understanding, although
inadequate attention is frequently paid to this fact in the

B

planning of educational services.  In addition to the greater-
than-previously-acknowledged competence of young children, it
is important to notice that recent psychological research has
demonstrated the significance of early childhood as a crucial
stage of development in a variety of domains including, among
others,intellectual development (e.g., Hunt, 1973), attention,
concentration and alertness (e.g. Kessen, 1967), cognitive
growth (e.g. Bruner, 1968; Inhelder & Piaget, 1958), and social
development (e.g., Baumrind, 1967).  Bloom (1976) reviewed some
of the major studies in the area and concluded that, between
the ages of about 2 and 10, children develop cognitive capacities such as language and skill in learning from adults, and
socio-affective properties such as need achievement, attentive-
ness and good work habits.  Thus, the early years lay down a
basis on which later psychological development builds -- indeed,
to some extent the degree to which later experiences are capable
of modifying development is a function of the foundation which
has been laid down by early experience.  Young children are not
only *ready* to benefit from an educative environment, but they
*need* stimulating experiences of an appropriate kind, if later
development is to follow an optimal course.
      A discussion of what this means for education is to be
found in the socalled "Worth Report" (Worth, 1972), prepared
under the auspices of the Government of the Canadian Province
of Alberta.  Worth argues that education should not be denied
to the under-six, and recommends the establishment of formal
systems of early education (which he calls "Early Ed").  He
outlines three main goals for Early Ed, including provision of
stimulation, fostering of a sense of identity, and provision of
appropriate socialization experiences (p. 50).  However, the
most important aspect of the Worth recommendations, for the
present purposes, is that he specifically rejects the notion
that early education should be a downward extension of existing
systems.  Its main function would not be the provision of preliminary academic training.  On the contrary, advocating early
education as the first stage in a system of lifelong education,
he suggests that its goals should include those of developing
skills for dealing with information and symbols, promoting appreciation of various modes of self-expression, nurturing curiosity and the ability to think, cultivating each child's confidence in his ability to learn, fostering a sense of self-
worth, and finally, increasing the capacity to live with others.
He thus sees early education as involving a complex of cognitive, motivational and socio-affective variables which, if appropriately developed, would serve as the basis for a lifetime
of self-fulfilment.  In so doing, he recognizes the importance

of education prior to conventional school age as one phase of
lifelong education.

## A CHANGED CONCEPTUALIZATION OF EDUCATION

*The role of school*

The development of wide-spread, state-supported school
systems in Europe and North America was, especially in the early stages, invariably accompanied by utilitarian values emphasizing practical learning. The main business of education was
considered to be the learning of certain basic skills which
would subsequently be of practical value in the life both of the
individual and of the society (e.g., Lynch & Plunkett, 1973).
More recently, however, educational values have started to shift
towards greater emphasis on the acquisition of social skills,
ethical values, healthy personality, and so on (e.g. Silva,
1973; Coles, 1972). As has been pointed out previously, school
training is seen by various writers as currently in process of
moving into areas traditionally regarded as the domain of the
family (e.g., Aujaleu, 1973; Coleman, 1972).

Despite the obvious relationship of schooling and learning
(which will be pursued more fully in the next chapter), it is
clear that learning is not confined to the periods spent in
school, nor even to the school years. For example, a very
great deal of the social learning people do occurs during adult
life, long after traditional schooling has been completed. Similarly, human infants who have not yet reached school age successfully carry out an enormous learning task which includes,
for example, the acquisition of the mother tongue, control of
sensory-motor systems, and so on. A great deal of this learning occurs in very early life (see Stone, Murphy & Smith, 1972,
for example). Nonetheless, in North American-European, highly-
developed societies, current practices in the provision of
learning facilities clearly rest on a belief that the best ages
for learning are between about 6 and 18, and that schooling during that period can meet all the formal learning needs of all
people for their entire lives. Furthermore this point of view
has often been "inherited" from former colonial powers by developing nations.

It is also apparent that the skills which have traditionally been emphasized in schools have been cognitive in nature,
with minimum emphasis on socio-affective skills, ethics, morals,
emotions and feelings, as has already been pointed out. Even
within the cognitive domain, emphasis has been one-sided. Learning, recognizing, recalling and reproducing information have

been stressed rather than methods of obtaining information,
skills in setting goals, techniques for communicating knowledge,
and related skills. At the same time, too little attention has
been paid to the wide spectrum of ways in which individual children differ from each other.  The consequent standardization of
schooling has involved the assumption that a narrow range of
relatively homogenized experiences is sufficient to cope with
the differences between students in their abilities, the needs
they have of education, their emotional attitudes to schooling,
their cognitive and social development, and so on.  A recent
analysis of the role of these latter kinds of factors in school
learning has been made by Bloom (1976).  In particular he has
emphasized the importance of individual differences in socio-
affective variables, and the need for highly differentiated
teaching of different children.

*Primacy of schooling*

As a result of the factors discussed in preceding paragraphs, three major assumptions about schooling have traditionally been paramount.  The first of these is that schooling
should be an intensive process, conducted during a relatively
short time-span.  This is, of course, the period of conventional schooling.  The second assumption is that, during this period of intensive management of learning, children should be
taught at least the bases of everything that they will need to
know when they become adults.  These first two assumptions partly arise from economic factors, such as the inability of earlier
industrial societies to finance extremely long periods of
schooling, and the need for skilled workers who enter industry
at a relatively early age already well-equipped with job-appro-
priate skills, and then spend the balance of their lives applying those skills.  They are also supported by sociological
and psychological observations indicating that children seem to
learn with far greater willingness and speed than adults,
in the normal course of events, and that children are much more
amenable to regimentation than adults.  As will be shown later,
the "scientific" basis for these kinds of belief may be relatively limited, but they are strongly entrenched in informal,
socio-psychological traditions.  Certainly, the tremendously
rapid and apparently effortless learning displayed by young
children as they acquire the habits and behaviour patterns of
their cultures is striking informal evidence of the ease of
learning in children.
    Associated with these first two assumptions, and possibly

arising from them, is a third -- the belief that school is the
paramount arena in which learning occurs during childhood and
early adolescence. With the development of a corps of professional teachers, it has traditionally been accepted that school
is the proper place for learning to go on. This has led to a
down-grading or ignoring of methods of learning and locations
of learning experiences which lie outside the classroom. With
the rise of the view that schools and schoolteachers are the
most important, if not the only, agencies of education in modern societies, the educational potential of other sources of
learning such as museums and libraries, the home, the place of
work, and so on, have been seriously neglected. The same applies to methods of learning such as self-directed learning,
"inter-learning" (learning in which learners learn from each
other rather than from an authoritative source), and similar
non-school-centred learning. As a result, learning has come to
be regarded as not really a part of ordinary life, but something which is done in special places that are removed from the
mainstream of life. /Similarly, since the main purpose of
schooling is to prepare people for the future, learning has
come to be seen as something which is only marginally relevant
to the real lives of learners.7 The rewards of today's learning
are traditionally thought to lie in tomorrow's increased well-
being. This divorce of school learning from real life has been
neatly summarized in the statement (Livingstone, 1943, p. 43)
that "youth *studies* but cannot *act*; the adult must *act* but has
no opportunity of *study*".

## The contrary view -- vertical and horizontal integration

Clearly, then, education has traditionally been conceptualized as remote from the facts of everyday life. Furthermore,
it has been seen as something which goes on in schools under
the direction of specialists. However, in recent years two
notions have received considerable stress: "horizontal integration" and "vertical integration". The arguments are different-
ly expressed by different writers, but a common set of ideas
can be discerned. The key notion of horizontal integration is
that education in the sense of school learning should be co-
ordinated with other components of society in which learning
occurs. Examples of such other components would be the home,
clubs and societies, places of work, interactions with peer
groups, and so on. Furthermore, it is argued that a very wide
range of the members of society should be involved in education,
and that knowledge itself should be seen as a broad integrated

network, rather than a series of more or less unrelated, narrow
and discrete disciplines. (Among other things, this latter
point suggests that school subjects should be treated as closely inter-related.) Thus, horizontal integration of education
means that the kinds of knowledge obtained outside the school
should not be regarded as separate from the kinds of knowledge
obtained in school, that the processes through which learning
goes on should not be divided into school-like and non-school
processes, and that all knowledge should be regarded as a continuous fabric.

Recent writings about education also involve certain beliefs about how it should be organized longitudinally over time.
Basic to these arguments is the view that learning goes on
throughout life, and that people are capable of learning at all
ages. This view is, of course, quite contrary to existing ster-
erotypes like "you can't teach an old dog new tricks", and to
many pronouncements in the area, such as William James's view
that anyone over the age of 25 has great difficulty in carrying
out new learning. It is increasingly being emphasized in modern writing that learning at any age level is a partial result
of prior learning, and that it partially regulates the nature
and extent of future learning. Hence, it is argued that this
longitudinal inter-relationship of learning across all age levels should be specifically recognized and utilized in educational organizations. This view involves endorsement of the principle of vertical integration.

Arguments of this kind have been reviewed and summarized
by Blakely (1972, pp. 105-109). He supports the view that it
is incorrect to regard education and schooling as synonymous
processes, pointing out that a high proportion of educative
learning goes on prior to the commencement of schooling or subsequent to its termination, that schooling is only one educative
influence in life, and that schooling is incapable, by itself,
of providing all the education needed for life. For these reasons he criticizes the isolation of schooling and the prevailing faith in formal schooling as the primary source of educative experiences. The most rapid and enduring changes during
the process of personal development take place prior to the
commencement of formal schooling. The longest period of life
by far is the one that commences after formal schooling ends.
Finally, the most powerful influences on growth, even during
formal schooling, come from outside schools (e.g., the media,
peers, the family, the community, and so on). Changed concepts
of the relationship between schooling, learning and education
are therefore needed.

It is apparent, then, that a new conceptualization of the

educational process is emerging.  In particular this conceptualization challenges the traditional faith in the primacy of
schooling and the relative detachment of schooling from life.
Furthermore, it urges the integration of the kinds of managed
learning referred to in the present chapter as "schooling" with
the kinds of informal learning which go on throughout life,
with or without deliberate management, with or without conscious awareness that learning is taking place.  Finally, the
changing conceptualization emphasizes the interactive nature of
learning over a lifetime, and the necessity for learning to
continue well beyond conventional school years, if successful
adjustment to the rapid changes of modern life is to be
achieved.  It is these kinds of view which lie at the heart
of the concept of lifelong education.

# Chapter 3

# Lifelong Education and Psychology

## EDUCATION, SCHOOLING, AND LEARNING

### *Education and learning*

The process of education may be very broadly defined as involving changes in understanding the external world, oneself, and one's relationship to people and objects in the environment. These changes facilitate interpretation of experience and permit increasingly effective behavioural techniques for dealing with life, making it possible, to some extent, to control those elements of the environment with which one comes into contact (Blakely, 1972). As Dewey (1916, pp. 90-91) defined it, education is "that reconstruction or reorganization of experience which adds to the meaning of experience and which increases ability to direct the course of subsequent experience." Thus, education is closely connected with learning: learning is the process through which education occurs. However, as Blakely (1972, p. 105) has put it, education in its broadest sense is a process of self-initiated, self-directed learning. It is engaged in spontaneously and naturally, without even the necessity of conscious awareness (Stephens, 1967). Education is therefore not synonymous with learning, especially learning of the formal kind.

### *Schooling and learning*

Schooling and learning are also closely linked: school is still overwhelmingly associated with learning, even though writers in the area may disagree concerning the particular kinds of learning which should be paramount. However, they are not the same thing. For example, learning need not be deliberately pursued, nor need learners even be specifically aware that they

are learning. Psychologists recognize the existence, for
instance, of "incidental learning", in which what is learned
may be acquired more or less accidentally, and without the
awareness of the learner. This kind of learning would not be
thought of as schooling (although it may, of course, occur during schooling, to the delight or dismay of educators). The
kinds of learning involved in schooling thus have certain features which distinguish them from the everyday learning that
occurs merely in living and developing. What gives schooling
its peculiar and unique relationship to learning is the fact
that, in the process of schooling, a deliberate and systematic
attempts is made to change behaviour through learning (Duke,
1976; Rohwer, 1970). To put it plainly, schooling involves a
set of procedures deliberately contrived for the purpose of
influencing the process of learning, in a particular way selected by the person directing the schooling. This direction of
the learning process is achieved through management of the circumstances in which the persons being schooled find themselves.

In formal schooling the attempt to modify learning is for
malized and standardized. It involves agents who are specifically  assigned the task of controlling learning (teachers),
learners who are at least partly aware of the fact that they
are engaged in the process of learning (the students), and a
deliberate set of goals or ideals whose realization, it is
thought, will be facilitated by the particular patterns of management of the learning process selected. Among other things,
this presupposes the existence of people who know how to influence learning, what should be learned, and when it should be
learned. These people are professsional educators such as
teachers and administrators. In schooling, professional educators deliberately provide environmental conditions which
they believe will alter learning, in order to achieve goals
which they regard as desirable. Thus, the relationship between
schooling and learning centres on the fact that, although
learning is lifelong and ubiquitous, it is only during schooling that a massive, state-funded, usually compulsory, systematic attempt is made to modify and regulate it.

*Education and schooling*

The term "education" is frequently used in juxtaposition
to statements about schools and schoolteaching. However, it
can quite correctly be more broadly understood as including the
full range of educative experiences people undergo in the normal course of their lives. Indeed, the possibility of receiving

an education through experience of life (education "in the
school of life") or, conversely, of having spent many years at
school but still being poorly educated in the life sense (the
"educated idiot"), is widely recognized in the vernacular expression of the everyday world.  Education and schooling are
linked by a common concern with learning, but they are not the
same thing (e.g., Duke, 1976).  Education is a more general
process, and does not result solely from contact with schools.
Schooling is thus merely a special instance of education.  This
point is crucial for understanding the principles of lifelong
education.  The distinction made here between education and
schooling may be regarded as forced, since the terms are often
treated as synonyms.  Nonetheless, it is important to notice
that the learning which goes on in school is only an example of
the natural, normal and everyday learning that occurs during
the broader process of education.  Furthermore, schooling is
only one of the many educative processes operating in life, and
school only one of the many educational facilities available.
This point of view is one of the major principles of lifelong
education.

*The concept of learning*

Emphasis throughout this book on learning as the core of
all education, both in and out of school, and as the very heart
of schooling, may create some problems for the reader.  It
should therefore be stressed that learning is meant to be understood in the broadest sense.  It is not meant to include changes
resulting from sheer physical growth, from contact with noxious
stimuli such as disease-bearing microorganisms, from physical
injury, and so forth.  However, the term is used in this book
to refer to a wide variety of psychological reorganizations
resulting from experience.  Such "psychological reorganizations"
clearly involve more factors than simply the particular patterns of reinforcement operating at the time they occur.  They
involve cognitive factors like interpretation of information,
appropriateness of input to existing levels of development, and
so on.  They also involve the presence or absence of appropriate
patterns of motivation, and a whole cluster of affective variables such as attitudes to the persons and materials involved,
and similar factors.

Furthermore, the concept of learning employed here is also
broad in a second sense.  Learning is taken to include acquisition of new social skills, development of changed attitudes
towards oneself and others, changed capacity to experience and

tolerate emotions, development of goals and aspirations, and so
on. This kind of conceptualization of the learning process has
been spelled out more fully by Blakely (1972). Although it is
true that learning is a process of adaptation to the environment, it is more clearly understood, especially in the context
of educative learning in humans, when it is borne in mind that
it is a *dynamic* process. Humans learn what aspects of experience to attend to and what tactics and techniques to employ for
interpreting experience. They learn how to learn, when to learn
and whether to learn. Learning, then, is not passive, but con-
sist of a "creative" process of selection and reorganization.
The mind can thus be thought of as "an instrument for learning"
(Blakely, 1972, p. 167).

Learning as it is conceptualized in the present text is
therefore a process of change in many aspects of psychological
life. When teachers talk about fostering the growth of self-
confidence, building skills in co-operating with others, developing positive attitudes towards learning materials, or similar
goals, they are really referring to their desire to facilitate
learning in these areas. In this sense lifelong education is
primarily concerned with learning, as is any educational system.
To sum up, organization of the book's argument around the central core of learning, as the process is understood here, in no
way implies concentration on education as a narrow process restricted solely to acquisition of knowledge of a scholarly, professional, or vocational kind. It includes such elements, of
course, but also concerns itself with motivational, cognitive,
affective, ethical, aesthetic and personal growth.

## *Lifelong education and lifelong learning*

An extension of the distinction between education and
learning is useful at this point -- the distinction between
lifelong *education* and lifelong *learning*. As has already been
shown, learning and education are not synonyms, and neither are
education and schooling. It has also been argued that learning
is already a life-long process that goes on with or without
schooling, and regardless of the kind of schooling that is received. As pointed out, the special characteristic of schooling is that it involves the deliberate provision of conditions
that will facilitate certain kinds of learning. Thus, lifelong
education is a goal or ideal which includes principles for organizing schooling to facilitate the process of lifelong learning, and to influence it according to special goals and ideals.
One aim of lifelong education is therefore to modify schooling

in order to shape and influence the kinds of learning that occur throughout life.  A school system organized according to
the principle of lifelong education would not *cause* lifelong
learning (it goes on already), but it would involve a deliberate attempt to influence the form, degree and quality of that
learning.


## PSYCHOLOGICAL BASIS OF EDUCATION

*Assumptions and beliefs underlying schooling*

       The institutionalization of education in schools involves
a standardization and homogenization of the educational processes experienced by children attending school.  This standardization both arises from and also helps to confirm conventional
beliefs about how learning goes on, what ought to be learned,
when it ought to be learned, and so on.  In fact, the deliberate
setting up of educational goals always involves adoption or
endorsement of certain beliefs of a psychological, economic,
socio-political, and sociological nature.  These beliefs may be
explicitly stated, as in preambles to some curricula, or they
may be implicit and scarcely recognized by those operating
within the system.
       This means that lifelong education too has associated with
it a set of beliefs of a psychological kind, in the same way as
such beliefs are associated with conventional schooling, although the precise nature of the beliefs may be different.  Endorsement of lifelong education pre-supposes that people ought
to learn in certain ways, under certain conditions, and for
certain purposes, and that this should go on throughout their
lives.  It also presupposes the existence of people who know
what these ways should be, and what the goals of learning are.
Indeed, one of the purposes of the present text is to make some
suggestions, based on current psychological knowledge, about
how lifelong education should be structured in order to influence lifelong learning.  However, any such recommendation involves a set of beliefs about what people should be like, what
sort of goals they should seek, what an "ideal" human being is
like, and so on.  It is well to bear this fact in mind.


*Psychological factors in the classroom*

       Education and psychology are deeply interrelated.  Clear
recognition of this fact is to be seen in the central role giv-
en to the study of psychological factors in programmes of teach-

er education.  The relationship is, however, complex, as Rohwer
(1970) has pointed out, and has not resulted in as fruitful a
collaboration as might have been expected.  Nonetheless, education is heavily concerned with learning and with modification
of the outcomes of learning in schoolchildren.  Education in
schools is also concerned with the management of the environmental factors in the classroom which foster learning.  It involves the establishment of "...conditions that explicitly direct the child towards intellectual activity in a relatively
regular and orderly manner" (Rohwer, 1970, pp. 1379-1380).  However, these conditions go far beyond merely provision of schedules of reinforcement which increase the likelihood that certain
responses will appear more frequently in the future, others less
frequently, while the conditions which foster learning in the
classroom include factors like level of difficulty and organization of material.  Thus, management of classroom learning involves a base of knowledge in the area of *cognitive psychology*.

In addition, learning in the classroom is heavily dependent
upon the establishment of appropriate *motivational climates*.
Although not normally reported in this way in the literature,
the behaviour of even the laboratory rat shows elements of intention and purpose.  In the case of the human child who is
learning in the classroom, a major factor in efficient learning
is a desire to learn.  But the development of positive motivation for learning is itself a psychologically complex phenomenon.  It involves what might be called "structural" features,
such as acceptance by the child that the material which is being
learned is in some way worthwhile.  The cry that classroom material is not "relevant", or that it has no application to the
child's real life, is an example of focus on this issue.  On
the other hand, positive motivation also involves what might be
called "process" variables, such as a desire to please a well-
liked teacher.

Finally, learning in the classroom arises from a cluster
of what will here be called "*socio-affective variables*". This
domain includes factors such as acceptance by children that
schooling is something from which they can benefit (rather than,
for example, a process which is imposed on them by some anony-
mous body like "the Government", with their compliance guaranteed by policing of Truancy Acts).  The socio-affective domain
also includes issues such as whether children see in the teacher
an ally or an aloof "toff", and whether they find the process of
learning exciting and stimulating, or boring, or even frighten-
ing.  Thus, the socio-affective factors in classroom learning
involve the question of whether or not children feel that they
are among friends in the classroom, that learning is a natural

and easy thing to do, that the teacher is an ally and friend, that school is a valuable tool in life, and so on. It could be summarized by saying that the socio-affective domain is concerned with the question of whether or not children feel that they belong to the classroom and that it belongs to them.

*Psychological factors in educational goals*

The successful management of classroom learning is a phenomenon in which the psychological elements are of profound importance. However, the psychological basis of education is by no means confined to the management of classroom learning. As has already been pointed out in Chapter 2, a major element of formal schooling is its deliberate management of children's experiences during the process of formal schooling, in order to achieve certain desired changes in behaviour. In other words, an understanding of the goals which underly what goes on in the classroom is an important factor in the analysis of education. In modern educational systems, these goals can usually be seen quite clearly in formally established curricula. Indeed, many curriculum documents are preceded by a formal statement of the purpose of the curriculum. These purposes are frequently stated in psychological or quasi-psychological language. For example, a typical curriculum preamble might state that a major purpose of teaching a particular subject in a particular school system is "to develop greater understanding of the logical basis of mathematical processes," or "to foster confidence in handling numerical operations."

In the early stages of development of widespread state-supported systems in Europe and North America, the main goal was usually utilitarian, in that the aim was to produce persons who would fit well into the society, or who would be well-equipped with the skills needed to function successfully in the society. The key requirements were usually possession of knowledge and training which would ensure gainful employment, or at least possession of the basic skills necessary for acquisition of job credentials in later life. But, even here in educational systems aimed at producing graduates who would be readily employable and self-supporting, a strong psychological basis can be discerned. It was, for example, clearly understood that students would have to be equipped with basic skills of a kind which would enable them, if necessary, to master unfamiliar material, even after leaving school. Consequently, theories were developed concerning just what kind of school experiences would produce individuals most skilled in learning. These theories were frequently couched in explicitly psychological terms such as the concept of "tranfer of training", which was supported by a body of psychological experimentation appearing to show that intensive training in a particular area subsequently led to an improvement of learning abilities in other areas, through a transfer effect.

It is very important to notice that such goals, even when they are said to arise from "scientific" evidence, depend very heavily upon socio-political factors such as the prevailing beliefs about heredity and environment in human development. For example, it is scarcely surprising that in 19th century British education transfer of training was widely accepted as a key psychological concept, since the socio-political view of the time was that differences between people were almost entirely a result of heredity which transmitted a general superiority or inferiority. To give an instance, Galton (1883) interpreted his statistics concerning the distribution of superior vocational achievement in England as evidence that "genius" ran in families and that it was of a highly general nature. He came to this conclusion when he noticed that, although the sons of "eminent" men were very frequently eminent themselves (inheritance of superiority), a son might become eminent in any one of a variety of fields, and not merely the field in which his father had been eminent (general nature of inherited genius). This point is raised here because it is of major importance to realize that more recent interpretations of psychological data, and consequent promulgation of "scientific facts", are just as likely to be affected by current socio-political thinking as were the conclusions of earlier educators.

## Educational goals in recent times

Although earlier statements of educational goals clearly had a psychological basis and rested on a body of psychological knowledge (bearing in mind that the interpretation of this knowledge was heavily affected by socio-political factors), it is only in more recent writings that an explicitly psychological turn has been given to statements about educational goals. Particularly in the face of the uncertainties that were emphasized in Chapters 1 and 2 about the nature of the world of the future, recent writers have dwelt more and more heavily upon the role of education in fostering certain patterns of psychological growth in children. Thus, the emphasis in statements of educational goals has switched from the acquisition of skills and knowledge to the production of a certain kind of people func-

tioning psychologically in a particular manner.  More recently,
emphasis has shifted further towards acquisition of social
skills, development of ethics and concern for others, development of a healthy personality, achievement of self-fulfilment,
and so on (e.g., Silva, 1973; Coles, 1972).  It has, in fact,
become explicitly apparent in recent writing about educational
goals that the goals are psychological in nature.  The relationship between psychology and education has thus become more and
more specific.  The processes and content of schooling are
based on psychological beliefs about how learning occurs and
what should be taught.  In addition, the goals of education are
based on psychological beliefs about what people need if they
are to live satisfactory lives, what constitutes a satisfactory
life, and so on.


## EVALUATING LIFELONG EDUCATION

In view of the argument that has just been developed, it
is clearly possible, and even desirable, to analyze education
from the point of view of the psychological assumptions underlying its structures, processes and goals.  Indeed, much of the
analysis of contemporary education presented in Chapter 2 and
contrasted with the assumptions of lifelong education had a
psychological base.  Education is, in fact, a psychological
process.  This is not to deny that it also has economic aspects,
administrational elements, sociological features, and so on.
For example the question of how classrooms are organized is an
administrative and economic issue as well as a psychological
one.  Nonetheless, as has been shown, there are psychological
elements at the very heart of the educational process, and it
is with these that the present text is concerned.


*Education and ideology*

Accepting the view just advanced that education is very
largely concerned with a set of psychological factors, the
evaluation of an educational system may clearly be based on
psychological criteria.  This precisely is the goal of the present book.  However, any evaluation of education (psychological
or otherwise) is immediately confronted with the practical problem of how to carry it out.  Educational goals are invariably
stated as sets of ideals.  Even where attempts are made to describe expected outcomes in some detail, the descriptions are
couched in abstract terms.  Thus, a typical aim for an educational curriculum would be stated in terms like "production of

students who are better equipped to function as citizens," or
"development of critical and logical thinking in students".
None of these descriptions is operational in the sense that a
statement like "development of students who borrow between 3
and 5 books from a library in any given week," is.

Even the psychological goals of education are normally
stated in the form of abstract ideals. Furthermore, these ideals tend to have a distinctly socio-political aspect, as has
already been pointed out. Thus, in a society which places high
value on conforming to the societal norms of good citizenship,
the ideals of education will be full of abstract statements
concerning the role of schooling in fostering "good citizenship". Such statements abound in curricula and educational
text books written in the United States during the 1950s. By
contrast, societies which at a particular time in their development revere abstract scholarship, will develop educational
goals emphasizing perfect knowledge of content areas which are
deemed to be representative of high scholarship (such as Latin,
Greek and Mathematics in 19th century England). Societies
which emphasizes co-operativeness, non-competitiveness, and
reverence for the State will emphasize educational ideals along
those lines, whereas societies in which the prevailing ethos
favours individualism, competitiveness and entrepreneural activities will build these social beliefs into their educational
goals.

In fact, then, educational goals are highly ideological in
nature. Far from being concrete, operational and universal,
they are intangible, idealistic and highly susceptible to the
popular ideologies of the time. As can readily be seen from
an examination of statements about educational goals in recent
years, accepted goals mirror the prevailing ideology of the
period when curriculum-developers were receiving their own education, while the competing pronouncements of educational ren-
egades urge curricula developed in terms of ideologies which
are, for their society, "advanced", "radical", "progressive",
and so on. Consequently, it is of great importance to understand that the idea of lifelong education is (a) an abstract
goal or ideal, (b) modified by current ideology or, at the very
least, socio-political beliefs in the societies to which its
proponents belong, (c) abstract and idealistic in the way it is
stated, rather than specific and operational.

*Problems of evaluating curricula*

This state of affairs is by no means confined to lifelong

education.  As has already been argued, curriculum innovations
in recent years have all had similar properties.  As a result,
a special problem that arises in evaluating any principles for
organization of education is how to evaluate a set of abstract
and idealized goals, which are not so much the result of a set
of objective, scientific discoveries, but of the socio-political
or philosophical persuasions of their proponents.  As with other
curriculum innovations, lifelong education as a goal or ideal
does not lead directly to changes in classroom procedures, while
to complicate matters further, the evidence that particular
classroom innovations have any major effects on children (whether they are introduced on the basis of a desire to foster lifelong education or not) is equivocal, to say the least.  Indeed,
some empirical findings have suggested that the connections between changes in classroom organization and changes in pupil
outcomes are slight (e.g., Jansen, Jensen and Mylov, 1972; Soar,
1972).  The recent report by Jenks and his colleagues (1972)
has strongly suggested that factors like family background and
personality are at least as important as school-related factors
in determining outcomes of schooling.  On the other hand, on
the basis of an extensive empirical study, Bennett (1976) has
concluded that teaching style was a significant determinant of
pupil achievement.
     The evaluation of particular educational practices is also
made difficult by the fact that changes in classroom procedures
will presumably have their most pronounced effects in the later
adult lives of students who experience them (since schooling is
supposed to prepare students for life).  Thus, evaluation of
the outcomes of teaching procedures would ideally require a
study covering at least one entire generation.  In fact, since
presumably the full effects would not be seen in children who
grew up in a world still dominated by the procedures followed
in the preceding generation, a hundred years or more might be
required for a true evaluation study to be carried out.  What
this means, in effect, is that attempts to evaluate changes in
educational procedures are always inadequate.  Furthermore, it
is probably a mistake to place too much emphasis on the pronouncements of scholars and reformers.  The ultimate decisions
may rest on the decisions, not necessarily taken on educational
grounds, of politicians or civil servants.  Innovations may
even be largely evaluated in terms of what the public will tolerate in schools (Duke, 1976).  Thus, evaluation may be based
largely on the subjective feelings about the new procedures of
teachers and students, or other observers such as politicians,
parents and employers, rather than on "scientific" findings.
On the other hand, evaluation may be more a matter of observa-

tion of later real-life problems, although again in an informal way. An example is the increasing resistance in some countries to "advanced" methods for the teaching of mathematics, which some employers (rightly or wrongly) are now claiming leave students unable to function in the business world, some parents are vociferously rejecting on the grounds that their children lack traditional basic skills, and some politicians are criticizing because they are said to be unfair to certain social classes.

In view of this state of affairs evaluation of curriculum innovations requires a special technique. Procedures in which some change in treatment is carried out and some clearly-defined outcome measures are subsequently obtained, with a comparison between treated and untreated subjects, are impossible, partly because innovations tend to be introduced universally, or else in a haphazard fashion which precludes systematic evaluation, partly because the criteria are usually stated in abstract and highly idealized terms, and partly because long-term studies covering one or more lifetimes are really needed for adequate evaluation. Because of these kinds of factors, formal, apparently "scientific", evaluations of innovation can readily be shown to be methodologically flawed and incapable of proving anything. This has been demonstrated by some scholarly reactions to a recent study in Britain (Bennett, 1976) which purported to demonstrate that traditional teaching methods were superior to certain innovative procedures (see Gray and Latterly, 1976 for a typical analysis which concludes that the Bennett study is incapable of providing conclusive answers). The result is that an educational principle is usually accepted or rejected in terms of the extent to which it fits in with the pre-existing beliefs and attitudes of teachers, students, politicians and the general public (i.e., the extent to which it "makes sense" or "feels right"). Validation of educational procedures, is, as it were, normally carried out through studies of "construct validity" rather than studies of "predictive validity". Lifelong education does not appear to be any different from the usual.

*Lifelong education and psychological knowledge*

Accepting that educational innovations can legitimately be evaluated by analyzing the theoretical principles on which they rest, and showing that these make sense in terms of existing knowledge, leads to the view that lifelong education can be evaluated by asking to what extent its theoretical basis (one

might be tempted to say its ideology) makes good sense when
analyzed in terms of a separate discipline whose findings do
rest on at least a quasi-experimental, scientific basis.  Indeed carrying out such an analysis is the purpose of the present text.  If lifelong education can be shown to be highly consistent with psychological knowledge of human development, then
its validity will be greatly enhanced.  Strictly speaking, of
course, what is required is a series of predictive studies in
which operational goals are established, classroom procedures
are operationally described, and the correlation or lack of correlation between the two is subsequently established.  However,
as has been shown, this is both very difficult in terms of time,
money and organizational problems, and not normally regarded as
necessary.

Like any other principle of educational organization, then,
lifelong education is essentially a statement of ideals, rather
than a scientifically-proven process.  It involves a set of beliefs about the goals towards which education should aim, the
principles it should stress, and the kinds of people it should
help to develop.  As an educational goal, it is at least as
abstract as is, say, "justice" as a socio-legal ideal.  Whether
or not the idealized psychological goal of lifelong education --
a person who is confident, creative, intellectually able, personally autonomous, ethical, and so on -- is in fact ever at-
tainable is unknown.  Similarly, the connection between the
curriculum prescriptions which flow from a commitment to lifelong education (which will be spelled out in more detail in a
later chapter) and the desired outcomes has never been demonstrated.  Thus, even total acceptance of the goals described
in Chapters 1 and 2 would not automatically dictate practical
classroom procedures.  The task confronting practical curriculum developers, even after they accept the ideal of lifelong
education, is to turn the abstract goal into a set of concrete
classroom operations which they believe will achieve the goal.
Practical evaluation can follow only then.  A classical, hypo-
thetic-deductive process would require formulation of hypotheses
about the nature of the necessary curriculum, testing of the
relationship between these curricular features and later real-
life behaviour, and subsequent modification of those features
of the system which were shown to be ineffective.  Such systematic development would require a longitudinal study covering
generations, and as is usual in curriculum development, it has
not been carried out.

To recognize this is not necessarily to reject lifelong
education as a guiding principle for educational development.
Nonetheless, it is important to realize clearly that it is an

abstract concept involving abstract and idealized goals, whose
capacity to be realized is not known.  It also involves curricular prescriptions whose exact connection to the stated abstract ideals is not known.  In other words, the question of
what classroom procedures will develop graduates who do indeed
become lifelong learners has not been empirically tested. Neither has the even more basic question of whether people are actually capable of becoming lifelong learners in the sense that
this term is used by proponents of lifelong education. Adoption
of the principle of lifelong education is, then, partly an act
of faith, with a strong socio-political element.  What this
means is that the validation of lifelong education will necessarily involve validation of the basic principles upon which it
rests, in terms of empirical knowledge in other areas such as
psychology.  For this reason, it is of considerable importance
to demonstrate that the basic principles of lifelong education
are consistent with psychological knowledge about human development.

*Key concepts*

Four key concepts must be clarified at this point.  The
first of these is the concept of lifelong education itself. As
the basic interrelationship of schooling, learning, life, and
education has already been discussed in detail in earlier sections, another full analysis is not required in this context.
*Lifelong education* can be defined as a formal goal or ideal for
the organization and structuring of educative experiences. The
nature of the goal has been outlined in Chapter 1.  This organization and structuring will extend over the entire age range
from earliest life until old age.  It may require an institutional basis quite different from that underlying conventional
schooling.  From this point on, when the term "lifelong education" is used, it is to be understood in this sense (a goal or
ideal for guiding educational organization).  A second major
concept employed throughout the present text is that of "lifelong learning".  It is already apparent that learning occurs
throughout life, quite independently of the existence or not of
a concept of lifelong education.  However, for the present purposes, the label "*lifelong learning*" will be used to refer to
"managed" learning, analogous to conventional school learning
as we currently know it but occurring in response to "lifelong
education".  Thus, whenever the term *lifelong learning* is used
from this point on, it is very important to notice that it will
refer, not to the inevitable and natural process of learning

throughout life which clearly occurs regardless of school organization, but to learning in response to a conscious desire to
learn on the part of the learner and a conscious effort to provide conditions facilitating such learning on the part of educative agencies.

A closely related concept for the present purposes is that
of the "lifelong learner". Again, it is apparent that all people are in a certain sense lifelong learners, quite independently of the way in which schooling is organized in their society.
However, in the present text the term *lifelong learner* will be
used to refer to persons who are conscious of themselves as
learners throughout life, see new learning as the logical way
to handle problems, are highly motivated to carry out such
learning at all age levels, and welcome change and challenge
throughout life as providing opportunities for new learning.
The inter-relationship of lifelong education, lifelong learning
and lifelong learners is thus seen to involve the formal provision of educational systems (based on the goal of lifelong
education) which aim at fostering the development of people
(lifelong learners), who consciously and systematically respond
adaptively to the demands of their environments throughout
their lives (in a process of lifelong learning).

A final concept is of relevance at this point -- that of a
"lifelong education-facilitating curriculum". The key feature
of the theory of lifelong education as far as educational practitioners are concerned is its implications for the way in which
the actual practice of teaching should be carried out. Lifelong
education is the philosophy, orientation or ideal, lifelong
learners and lifelong learning are the hoped-for results, and a
*lifelong learning-facilitating curriculum* is the practical means
through which the results are to be achieved. This means that
the practical task facing curriculum developers is to design a
curriculum which implements the principles of lifelong education. The practical goal of researchers which would follow the
implementation of such a curriculum (a lifelong education-facilitating curriculum) would be the demonstration that the curriculum designed on lifelong education principles had indeed pro-
duced lifelong learners who subsequently engaged in lifelong
learning.

*Structure of the analysis*

The view that school learning is essentially a complex of
cognitive, motivational and socio-affective variables has already been stated. The psychological analysis of lifelong ed-

ucation which follows will be organized in terms of this three-
part framework.  In a nutshell, the aim is to show that the
implicit psychological assumptions underlying lifelong education in the areas of cognitive functioning, motivation, and
socio-affective functioning are "correct" in terms of contemporary psychological knowledge.  Correctness in this sense
would greatly increase the confidence with which changes in
educational organization, in terms of the concept of lifelong
education, would be implemented, while serious inconsistencies
between the basic concepts of lifelong education and current
psychological knowledge would greatly detract from the confidence with which educational administrators could implement it.
     At this point it is presumably not necessary to show that
the basic principles of lifelong education are more in accordance with psychological knowledge than those of conventional
education.  Since lifelong education contains a set of goals
which are discriminably different from those of education as it
is currently organized, merely showing that lifelong education
is in accordance with psychological knowledge would provide a
sufficient basis for further examination of the principle.  Acceptance or rejection would, presumably, then rest upon the acceptance or rejection of the stated goals of lifelong education.
This means, of course, that a thorough analysis of the legitimacy of lifelong education as an organizing principle, and decisions concerning whether existing school systems should be
modified in terms of the concept of lifelong education, will
not rest on the psychological analysis alone.  A "clean sheet"
psychologically speaking would merely legitimize further study
of the concept.  Although a demonstration of marked inconsistencies between the principles of lifelong education and psychological knowledge would presumably invalidate the principle
from further consideration, its acceptance would require a much
more complex analysis than the present one in terms of a much
wider range of disciplines such as economics, sociology, administration, and so on.  A commencement in this direction has
been made in Dave (1976).
     The analysis of lifelong education from a psychological
viewpoint also has an important second aspect, although this
element will be given less emphasis in the present text than
the first question (whether or not the basic rationale of lifelong education is psychologically well-founded).  This second
aspect concerns the implications of psychological knowledge for
designing a lifelong education-oriented curriculum.  Thus, the
psychological analysis of lifelong education has two forms.
The first of these is the application of psychological knowledge to the question of whether lifelong education "make sense".

The second concerns the matter of what a lifelong education-
oriented curriculum should be like in the light of contemporary
psychological knowledge.

Chapters 4, 5 and 6 will review psychological knowledge
concerning the interaction between life, experience and learning, and review the extent to which the principles of lifelong
education, as stated in Chapter 2, are consistent with that
knowledge.  Although it has already been argued that provision
of evidence for the effectiveness of a lifelong education-facilitating curriculum is not strictly necessary for an analysis of
the concept of lifelong education, and indeed such evidence is
not normally offered when any curriculum organization is evaluated, Chapter 7 will discuss the implications of the psychological analysis of lifelong education for curriculum design,
will indicate some of the broad properties of a lifelong education-facilitating curriculum, and will attempt to evaluate the
concept from this point of view.  Finally, Chapter 8 will crit-
ically evaluate the whole principle, primarily from a psychological point of view.

# Chapter 4

# The Persistence of Learning Throughout Life

PSYCHOLOGICAL ASSUMPTIONS OF CURRENT EDUCATIONAL ORGANIZATION

Current institutionalization of education provides schooling only in the years of childhood and adolescence. This conventional restriction of formal schooling to a period between the ages of about 6 and 18 may originally have arisen from primarily social and economic considerations. For example, parents would have experienced considerable hardship in supporting children engaged in full-time education until, say, the age of 30 or beyond. At the same time, the society's needs for workers would not have been met by a system which kept people engaged in full-time schooling into middle adulthood. Nonetheless, it is clear that the traditional organization of schooling is both supported by and supportive of a set of psychological beliefs about learning. Although it may not necessarily have been a major consideration in the development of schooling as it currently exists, current practices clearly reflect the conviction that the best ages for learning are those during which schooling now takes place.

Indeed, it is apparent that enormous amounts of material really are learned during the time span covered by conventional school ages. Observation of this fact gives strong support to the view that learning is best done during the age period in which school is now offered. However, the extent to which a teleological error has been committed is not clear. Thus, the fact that the largest readily observable learning tasks are successfully carried out during childhood and adolescence may be due, not to this being the best time to attempt such learning, but to it being the time during which the best learning opportunities are available.

There is ample evidence of the widespread belief that childhood and adolescence are the periods of life in which

53

school-like learning is most effectively carried out.  Writers
like William James and many since have concluded that in the
normal course of events, very little worthwhile is learned after
the age of about 25.  It has also been argued (e.g., Lehman,
1953) that creativity is normally exhausted by the age of 40 or
so.  Faith in the primacy of early life as a time for learning
is also exemplified by popular sayings like: "you can't teach
an old dog new tricks."  The purpose of the present chapter is
to examine the validity of this belief, i.e., whether or not
the age-span at which children normally attend school does indeed cover the ages at which learning ability is at its peak,
and whether people outside school age can learn.  *Can* you teach
an old dog new tricks?


## INTELLIGENCE AND AGE

*The growth of intellectual abilities*

   The conventional conceptualization of the developmental
curve for intellectual abilities is that there is rapid growth
in early life, a peak at a relatively early age, a plateau-
period of stability, and finally a rapid decline in late adulthood.  However, as McLeish (1963, pp. 68-69) has emphasized,
authorities have not been able to agree on the precise age at
which the period of rapid growth ends, the age at which rapid
decline sets in, and so on.  An extreme opinion about the developmental curve for the growth of intellectual abilities was
that of Pressey and Kuhlen (1951, p. 42) who concluded, although
they were referring to psychological growth in general, not
purely intellectual growth, that "...all types of growth go
forward relatively steadily and rapidly during the first 18 or
20 years then, rather quickly, all stop together".  Other estimates of the ages at which the peak functioning of intellectual
ability occurs have ranged from 13 (Doll), to 14 1/2 (Dearborn),
to 15 or 16 (Binet, Kuhlmann, Terman, Otis) and right through
the intervening ages to as high as 40 (Heinis).  Bayley (1955)
reported increases in abilities up to the age of 21, Wechsler
(1958) placed the upper limit of growth at between 25 and 30,
and Bayley and Oden (1955) concluded that the upper limit is
not reached until about age 50.
   Despite this disagreement concerning the exact age limits,
the relationship assumed to exist between age and intellectual
abilities has typically had the form of Figure 1, which is
shown below.  This kind of curve has been cited by Wechsler
(1958).

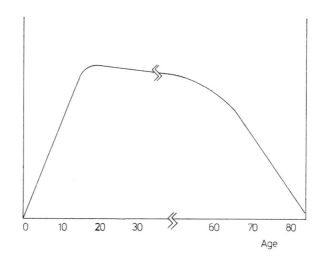

Fig. 1.   Stereotype of intellectual
growth and decline with age

        This opinion about the growth of intellectual abilities
gained support from several influential and widely-known studies
conducted between the two world wars.  It has continued to be
accepted until the very recent emergence of new interest in
adult intellectual functioning and adult abilities which started in about 1950 (Havighurst, 1969, p. 59).  The first of the
early "classical" studies was conducted by Yerkes (1921).  It
involved some 15,000 U.S. Army officers, ranging in age from 18
to 60, who were tested during World War 1.  Results of the
scores of the officers on a battery of abilities tests showed
that there was a steady decline in the average scores of the
age groups from the under-20s, to the early and late 20s,
through the 30s and 40s, and so on.  This led to the conclusion
that there was a fall-off in intellectual abilities from the
under-20s age group through the older age groups, the fall-off
increasing as the age of the groups increased.
        A similar large-scale, cross-sectional study of residents

of villages in New England (Jones & Conrad, 1933) divided the
New Englanders into groups of similar ages and calculated av-
erages on various ability tests for each of these age groups.
It differed from the Yerkes study in that the subjects included
children of below military age.  The mean scores for the various
age groups peaked at about age 20, then fell off steadily until
the mean for 55-year-olds was equal to that of 11-year-olds.
This finding was interpreted as indicating that the intelligence of 55-year-olds had fallen away from a peak at about age
20 until it had "deteriorated" to the level of 11-year-olds. A
somewhat similar but more recent cross-sectional study conducted in England (Vincent, 1952) also showed that there was a
steady decrement in age-group mean scores from 21 to 60.

These kinds of finding have contributed to the widely-
accepted view (especially among members of the public) that intellectual ability peaks in late adolescence and then falls off,
with severe decrements occurring in late adulthood and old age
(e.g. Granick and Freedman, 1973).  Such findings are, of
course, highly consistent with the existing practice of providing organized learning experiences during childhood, in order to stimulate the intellectual growth process which has been
shown to occur, and then terminating such stimulation in late
adolescence or early adulthood.  They also support the prevailing view that people beyond age 40 or so are not really capable
of acquiring new skills, or can only do so with great difficulty.

*Task-specificity and the growth of abilities*

Despite the kinds of data just cited, it soon became apparent that the generalized curve shown in Figure 1 was merely
an average, which masked both the extreme variability within
age groups (e.g., the brightest 50-year-olds obtained test
scores considerably higher than those of the dullest 20-year-
olds, despite the alleged mental deterioration of 50-year-olds),
and also the fact that the growth curve is different for different kinds of ability.  In fact, then, any decline in abilities which does occur is specific to certain kinds of ability
and not general to all abilities (e.g., McLeish, 1963, p. 1-9).
Several major summaries of the relationship between intellectual
abilities and age (e.g., Tyler, 1965; Anastasi, 1958) have reported that the fall-off is most marked in the kinds of ability tapped by tests of analogies, number series tasks, and reasoning tasks.  It is least marked, or even not present at all,
in tests of vocabulary and arithmetic.  More recent findings by

Schaie and Labouvie-Vief (1974) also reported that arithmetic
and word meaning skills persisted until at least the mid-50s.
Finally, Havighurst (1969, p. 60) concluded that there is a
fall-off in performance on tasks requiring speed and high levels of perceptual skills, but that there is no similar fall-
off in tasks requiring experience and "know-how", or on those
requiring vocabulary. Havighurst also concluded that what he
called "competence" to deal with life does not follow the stereotyped growth curve presented in Figure 1.

    Indeed, this was noticed even in the early studies previ-
ously cited. For example, the declines reported by Jones and
Conrad were greatest on tests of analogies, common sense, and
number series. There was no decline until the age of about 60
on tests of information and vocabulary. Foulds and Raven (1948)
showed that there was no decline in the vocabulary scores of
factory workers of differing ages, although there was a decline
on a reasoning test (Raven's Matrices). Again, although they
reported overall data supporting the generalized relationship
expressed in Figure 1, studies of Wechsler's subscales (e.g.,
Fox and Birren, 1950) indicated that elderly subjects got much
better scores on some kinds of tests than on others, and supported the argument that it is incorrect to speak of a general
and universal tendency for intellect to decay after adolescence,
although it may be true that there are some specific kinds of
tasks which are less well-performed by older people. This conclusion was supported by a study of Corsini and Fassett (1953)
which involved prisoners in San Quentin who ranged in age from
15 to 70. Older subjects surpassed younger ones on several
verbal abilities. Wechsler (1958) found it necessary to distinguish between "hold" abilities, which did not decline markedly with age, and "don't hold" abilities that did. As Tyler
(1965, p. 280) has concluded, there is overwhelming evidence
that some abilities at least remain stable or even increase up
to about age 60.

    An important recent review of evidence in this area is
that of Horn and Donaldson (1976). Although writing from the
point of view that the recent tendency has been to underesti-
mate the degree of age-related decrement in intellectual functioning, especially on the part of those with a vested interest
(such as writers in the area of lifelong education), they concluded that there is a need for caution in asserting that all
intellectual abilities decline with age, that some abilities
may not decline at all, and that whatever decline occurs may
not commence as early as has been thought to be the case. Finally, they pointed out that patterns of decline may be different for different people, or that they may not occur at all

for some people.

*Causes of task-specific deterioration with age*

It seems, then, that, despite the early stereotype that
the capacity to carry out intellectual tasks falls off with age,
no single general statement can adequately describe the relationship between age and task performance. On some tasks (especially those involving verbal skills) improvement may continue
more or less throughout life, while on others there may be an
extremely slow decline, or a position of stability may be reached and held until old age. It is true that on some kinds of
task, a performance decrement with old age may occur. However,
even where age-related fall-off in performance is reported, a
number of possible explanations exists. One of these is that
physiological deterioration occurs in the bodily systems involved in carrying out intellectual tasks. Welford (1969), for
example, has suggested that aging may be accompanied by a reduction in the nervous system's capacity to deal with stimuli,
as a result of physiological changes. Even here, however, he
has shown that where material is presented under appropriate
circumstances, the elderly may achieve good levels of performance. Thus, the possibility arises that, even if there is physiological deterioration, adults may successfully carry out
learning tasks given appropriate kinds of instruction and appropriate performance conditions.

This conclusion suggests that the techniques and skills of
youth may not be appropriate to middle and later life, and that
with advancing age there is a great need for people to mobilize
their intellect and organize their abilities in new ways, which
take advantage of "hold" or "continued growth" abilities to sup-
plement "don't hold" abilities. That is to say, there is a
need to approach tasks in new ways more appropriate to existing
patterns of abilities. This argument supports the view that
education should be lifelong, since it implies that new approaches to problems need to be adopted with advancing age, and
not that problems become insoluble as age increases. Indeed,
there is a good deal of evidence (reviewed in a later section)
which shows that even the elderly are capable of school-like
learning under appropriate instructional conditions. That intellect functions in qualitatively different ways at differing
ages does not, then, suggest that learning should necessarily
slow down beyond school age, but, rather, that opportunities to
learn should be patterned according to the changing nature of
intellectual abilities. This implies, in turn, that confining

schooling to a narrow age band is inappropriate.

*Role of motivation and attitude*

Quite apart from the question of whether age-related changes in patterns of intellectual functioning are a result of physiological factors, is the question to what extent such changes also reflect changes in affective variables such as motivation and attitude. In a very early study of intellectual functioning, Galton (1869) emphasized the importance of "zeal" in intellectual performance. Similarly, more recent writers like Cattell (in McLeish, 1963, p. 78) referred to the need for "tenacity" and "enterprise". Friend and Zubek (1958) concluded that older subjects obtained poorer scores because of lower "objectivity" (the tasks made them anxious) and "inflexibility" (they found it difficult to adopt new methods). Thus, they emphasized the effects of attitudes and emotional factors. Finally, it has been suggested by some psychotherapists that diminished capability of the elderly to cope, even when it takes the form of impaired memory, reduced alertness and less effective handling of life situations, may be conceptualized as the result of affective and motivational states rather than of failing capacities. Thus, the question arises of whether poorer performance of adults and the elderly on certain kinds of task may not result as much from reduced interest, low levels of motivation, negative attitudes towards learning and problem solving, and so on, as from impaired ability.

A recent summary of some of the findings concerning fall-off in the performance of the elderly by Schaie (1974) has reviewed the effects of a number of motivational-affective variables. Older people may, for example, feel embarrassed and nervous about their prospects of succeeding (especially if they have accepted the prevailing view that advancing age can be equated with decreasing competence). They may try to avoid tasks on which there is external supervision or pacing. Motivation to carry out intellectual tasks may be low: this is especially the case if it is borne in mind that the overwhelming orientation of intellectual test materials is towards the interests (as well as the skills and capacities) of the young. Consequently, a firm belief in the minds of adults that they are not supposed to be interested in learning, and that certain kinds of abilities are supposed to deteriorate, might be expected to lead to greatly reduced levels of performance on tests of intellectual abilities, reduced willingness to carry out new learning tasks, reduced interest in acquiring new skills and knowledge, and so on.


*Role of speed*

    One performance factor related to the motivational domain
is speed.  There is a body of evidence which suggests that apparent differences in the abilities of young and old human
beings are largely an artefact of differences in their abilities to work at high speed, rather than differences in the
underlying abilities involved.  For example, Welford (1969) has
reported that speed is impaired in the elderly and that, as a
result, accuracy suffers when they are required to work fast.
When high speed is not necessary for the solution of a task,
accuracy is not impaired.  He interpreted this as a result of
a general, biological decrement in the central nervous system,
rather than in terms of psychological factors like motivation
or interest.  On the other hand, Jerome (1962) reported performance decrements in the elderly somewhat similar to those
reported by Welford, but concluded that although they might
result from a loss in the physiological capacity to work at
high speed, they might also reflect a decrement in motivation.
    Canastrari (1963) and Eisdorfer (1965) have emphasized
the interaction among motivation, anxiety and speed.  Two factors may be involved (Schonfield, 1974); inability to disregard
irrelevant information unless time is available to sort things
out and distinguish between what is important and what is un-
important for the particular task in progress, and greatly increased cautiousness involving not only "looking before you
leap", as Schonfield says, but also looking while you are leap-
ing.  However, these problems are far less obvious when the
task is not subjected to external timing.  It is not that the
elderly cannot work at speeded tasks, but that they greatly
prefer self-pacing.  In any case, both a reduced physiological
ability to work at high speed and a more clearly psychological
distaste for working at high speed would be expected to interact
with psychological factors like confidence and enjoyment, to
yield performance decrements which are as much a result of the
psychological as of the physiological elements.  For example,
people who believed that high-speed work was difficult would
seek to avoid such work, often utilizing the socially-acceptable
explanation of advancing age to rationalize their behaviour,
whether or not any real biological decrement existed.  This acceptance of, or even utilization of, the popular stereotype of
the elderly as incompetent has been referred to by Gelpi (1976)
as a block to the establishment of lifelong education.

A major clarification of the role of speed in performance decrement in the elderly was made by Lorge (1936). He showed that the differences between elderly and youthful subjects which were present on speeded tests were not found on tests in which there were no time limits, a finding which is consistent with the conclusions of Welford and Schonfield. Lorge then extended his findings by calculating a "correction factor" to remove speed effects from differences in scores on ability tests. Subsequently, he applied this correction factor in a re-analysis of the seminal Jones and Conrad data already referred to in the previous section. The result of the correction for speed was that there were no longer any age differences in scores on the abilities test. Thus, there are grounds for concluding that speed is strongly implicated in apparent relationships between age and ability. Furthermore, even if such decrements are a result of physiological deterioration, they would be expected to interact with attitudinal and motivational factors to produce performance decrements, so that the decrements would not necessarily be permanent or irreversible.


*Effects of education*

A third factor affecting the relation between abilities and age is *education*. A classical study in this area is that of Miles and Miles (1932), which compared scores of various age groups divided according to educational level. This study suggested that the decay curve is identical for people of differing educational levels, and that it roughly followed the generalized pattern shown in Figure 2 on page 62. However, their data show that there are separate (although parallel) curves for subjects of differing educational levels. In fact, their 60-year-old university graduates obtained average scores superior to those of poorly-educated 20-year-olds. Tyler (1965, p. 282) reached a closely related conclusion in a summary of research in the area. However, she concluded that intelligence continues to develop for a longer period in the more highly educated than in the less educated, thus suggesting that the shape of the growth curve of intelligence is different for people of differing levels of education. Nonetheless, apart from the possibility that intellectual deterioration is longer delayed in those of higher education, there are grounds for believing that increased education has the effect of shifting the entire curve of intellectual growth and decay to a higher level. In Figure 2 which is shown below, the original Miles and Miles figure, the effect of higher education was apparently to move

c

Lifelong Education

the intellectual growth curve up the ordinate.

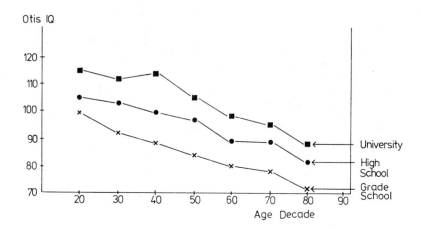

Fig. 2.  Age differences in intelligence test scores
         for groups reporting differing amounts of
         formal education


        A second education-related factor in the connection be-
tween intellectual abilities and age has been identified by
McLeish (1963, p. 71).  By comparison with adolescents or young
adults, the elderly are separated from their schooldays by a
considerably longer time period.  In fact, one may see in them
the effects of "rustiness".  As McLeish has concluded, citing
data like those of Sward (1945), continued exercise of school-
like skills results in a reduced tendency for them to deteriorate in old age.  This suggests that recent contact with
school or working in a setting in which abilities are frequently exercised results in less fall-off in those abilities with
advancing age.  Thus, findings connecting intellectual deterioration with schooling indicate that continued access to schooling results in improved mental functioning in the elderly.
This in turn suggests that contact with schooling throughout

life, such as would be seen in a lifelong-education oriented
system, would greatly improve intellectual functioning in
adults and the elderly.

*Longitudinal studies of age and intellectual functioning*
    Several methodological problems arise in investigating the
question of whether people's mental ability falls off with advancing age. One of these, whether conclusions about age and
intellectual functioning are confounded by non-intellectual
variables, has just been discussed. A second methodological
problem in the area involves the fact that all of the evidence
mentioned to date was derived from studies in which the differing age groups consisted of different people. Their performance was sampled at the same time. In other words, inferences
about abilities at age 60, for example, and their relationship
to those at, say, age 16, were made by testing a group of people currently 16 years of age and another group of people who
were currently 60 years old. Simply comparing the scores of
today's 60-year-olds with those of today's 16-year-olds involves the assumption that people who are now 16 will, in 44
years time, behave in much the same way as people who are now
60. This method of making inferences about psychological development is called the "cross-sectional" method.
    Although it eliminates the necessity to wait a lifetime to
find out what today's children will be like when they grow up
to become adults, the cross-sectional method thus rests upon a
very dubious assumption. For example, the extent to which the
two groups (today's 16-year-olds and today's 60-year-olds) had
the same opportunities for intellectual development are likely
to be very different. The younger group will probably have
been extensively exposed to the effects of television, have had
greatly increased opportunities for travel, have interacted
with relatively better-educated parents, and so on. Furthermore, a person born in 1958 will probably have stayed in school
much longer than the average person born in 1914, a factor
which has been argued in the previous section to be of considerable importance.
    Green (1969) has discussed some of these problems in a
study which attempted to disentangle some of the confounding
variables. In order to equalize level of schooling in a cross-
sectional study of adults and adolescents, he selected older
subjects in their 60s who had had as much schooling as the adolescents whom he studied. When this was done, differences between adolescents and elderly were very small, However, even

here, there was a methodological difficulty. Green's elderly
subjects were all characterized by a level of education which
was average for youngsters nowadays. However, in the 1920s
when they were actually at school, education at this level was
available only to a few adolescents. Thus, the two groups that
were supposedly "matched" contained adolescents of average
schooling on the one hand, and 60-year-olds of superior schooling, on the other. In all probability, then, the comparison
was between people who, as adolescents, had been rather bright
or else financially well off (otherwise they would not have
received advanced schooling), and present-day adolescents of
average ability. If it is also borne in mind that the elderly
people were the survivors of their age cohort, since the chron-
ically sick and similar groups would largely have died off before the study, a good performance on the part of the elderly
people is hardly surprising.

    What is needed, then, is evidence gathered from studies in
which the same group of people is examined at two different
points in time in order to see how they have changed over the
years. This approach requires what are called "longitudinal"
studies. One famous set of longitudinal studies was carried
out by Owens (see Owens, 1953; Owens and Charles, 1963). He
tested 127 men who had taken an intelligence test (Army Alpha)
in about 1920, carrying out the re-testing no less than 30
years later (Owens, 1953). He reported that their average total score was not lower, but higher. The same result was found
in a number of the sub-tests. In another study (Owens and
Charles, 1963), he retested men who had been drafted into the
U.S. Army during the first world war at an average age of 21,
40 years later when they were over 60 years old on average.
Again, no drastic fall-off in ability was seen. Similarly,
Campbell (1965) reported that a group of university students
he re-tested after a time lapse of 25 years gained higher
scores on a college entrance test at the re-test than they had
obtained on the first occasion.

    Such results are not confined to American samples. For
example, Nisbet (1957) re-tested a group of Scottish schoolteachers after the lapse of 24 years. He found that they obtained higher average scores on 13 of 14 sub-tests at age 46
than they had at age 22. Bradway and Thompson (1962) also
showed, although the age-span of their subjects was not so
large, that such findings are not confined to people with university training. Testing members of the public rather than
persons selected for high education, they found that the average IQ of their subjects increased by 11 points between the
first testing in 1941, when the subjects were between 12 and

17 years of age, and the second testing in 1956, when they were between 27 and 32 years old. Longitudinal studies still leave many questions unanswered, and are subject to many methodological difficulties (see Horn and Donaldson, 1976, for a discussion). However, they represent, by and large, an improvement on cross-sectional studies and, in contrast to cross-sectional studies, do not necessarily support the view that intellect deteriorates with advancing age. On the contrary, they often suggest that intellectual growth continues until well into life.

Taking such findings along with earlier discussions of factors contributing to the maintenance of high levels of intellectual functioning such as advanced schooling, positive attitudes towards learning and thinking, and the presence or absence of rustiness, these findings strongly suggest that the relative inability of the aged (if such an inability exists) could be greatly reduced by designing an environment in which contact with educative agencies continued throughout life, and in which people were encouraged to believe that they are capable of learning and change at all age levels -- the kinds of environment envisaged by proponents of lifelong education. As Pressey (1951) has pointed out, there are few educational opportunities adapted to the needs and circumstances of people of advanced years. There may well be those who wish to continue school-like learning, but are frustrated by awkward physical arrangements, inappropriate time schedules and uncomfortable social environments in existing facilities.

At the very least the evidence for a decline in intellectual ability with age is equivocal. There is a strong possibility that the widely accepted notion that age and intelligence are negatively correlated may be erroneous. Unfortunately, such a conclusion would tend to be self-perpetuating, since a firm belief on the part of adults and old people that they cannot learn would lead to negative attitudes towards learning, avoidance of new learning, unwillingness to make adequate efforts, and so on.

## Shifting baseline hypothesis

Despite this conclusion, findings in cross-sectional studies require some explanation. The purpose of the present section is to suggest one. Suppose that the growth of intellect with age is actually a matter of steady increase until at least age 40 or so. Hirt (1964), for example, has reported peaks in some abilities in the 30s, as has Schaie (1970). Suppose, additionally, that the baseline of the growth curve has

moved steadily upward over the last 50 years or so. (What is
meant by this is that, within a particular generation, the
developmental curve may be similar but that between generations
there may be an upward shift in what is normal and ordinary for
a person of a given age to be able to do.) If the growth
curves of ability for several generations are superimposed on
each other, as has been done in Figure 3, the curve which would
be obtained in a cross-sectional study would have the form of
the cross line, even where the "true" situation for members of
a particular generation was one of steady growth throughout
life. Although the hypothetical "true" curve involves continual albeit decelerating growth, the assumption that people now
10 give a representative score for 10-year-olds of all generations, that people now 20 give a representative score for all
generations, and so on, leads to the composite curve shown
superimposed on the hypothesized curves for six different generations. It is clear that this composite in no way summarizes
or fairly represents any of the individual generation's growth
curves. On the contrary, it seriously distorts the situation.
Cross-sectional studies may well have yielded just such a distortion.

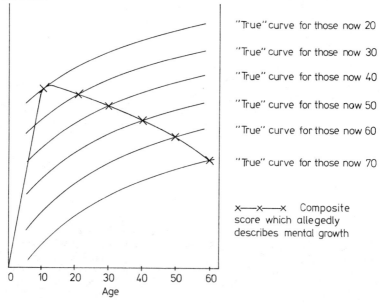

"True" curve for those now 20

"True" curve for those now 30

"True" curve for those now 40

"True" curve for those now 50

"True" curve for those now 60

"True" curve for those now 70

x—x—x  Composite
score which allegedly
describes mental growth

Fig. 3.  Effects of a baseline shift

A similar point has been made by Bromley (1974, p. 334).
Figure 4, taken from his book on human aging (p. 334), illus-
trates the way in which different conclusions might be drawn
from longitudinal and cross-sectional studies of the growth of
intellectual functions with age. Function A is one in which
there really is a decline with age. In this case, follow-up
studies (indicated by the solid line) and cross-sectional
studies (broken line) both correctly indicate that there is a
fall-off over time. Function B is one in which there is, in
reality, an improvement with time in each given individual, but
in which the initial level is higher in younger subjects than
in older ones. In this case, longitudinal studies would indicate improvement with age, cross-sectional studies deterioration with age.

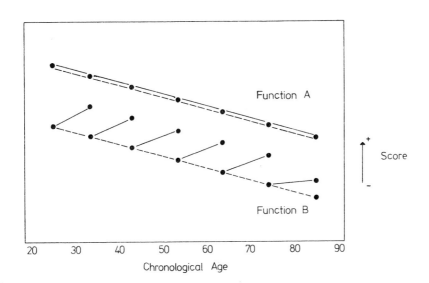

Fig. 4.  Discrepancies between longitudinal
         and cross-sectional studies

*Possible reasons why a base-line shift may occur*

The curves depicted in Figure 3 for each generation are purely hypothetical. There is no implication that they are necessarily actual representations of what the "true" growth curve for intellect really is. Indeed, as Tyler (1965, pp. 284-285) has pointed out, the actual shape of the growth curve for intellectual functioning is not known. Furthermore, there are tremendous problems associated with discovering what it is. For example, merely testing the same subjects twice, say at age 10 and again at age 60, does not indicate what the pattern of growth has been in between the two ages. Scores on intellectual tests may very well show an increase from age 10 to age 60. However, there is no evidence of whether the increased 60-year-old score represents a peak at that age, a point on an ascending curve, a point on a descending curve, or some other relationship with earlier scores. For example, it is conceivable that there may have been an earlier peak, and that the latest score is actually part of a decline. This state of affairs would not be demonstrated by the hypothetical procedure described, since the peak would have occurred at an age level not sampled in the study. Similarly, relative speeds of change between various ages not sampled would not be detected. What is needed is a long-term program of continuing assessment.

Such a programme would, however, pose new problems such as expense, need for patience, effects of familiarity with the procedures on test scores, and so on. A review of recent advances in research methodology in the area, and of the associated problems, is to be found in Horn and Donaldson (1976). Nonetheless, despite the difficulty of making definitive statements in the area, it seems safe to say that the truth of the belief that mental capacity declines with advancing age has not been unequivocally demonstrated. Furthermore, there are a number of grounds for viewing with suspicion the claim that such a decline does occur. The present hypothetical explanation of the findings obtained in cross-sectional studies, in terms of a shifting baseline, would be highly consistent with obtained data, assuming that succeeding generations developed mental skills more rapidly and to a higher level than earlier generations. This possibility is quite consistent with what is known about changing social conditions, and with hypotheses concerning the effects of early experience and attitudes on intellectual development, and emphasizes the importance of early education. A shifting baseline would also be expected if the skills acquired by younger subjects were more closely attuned to the demands of the test situation at the time testing occurred. In other words the skills of older subjects might simply become obsolete (Schaie, 1974). Again this suggests that continuing updating and re-education would foster improved performance in older people.

*Reasons for intergenerational changes*

One classical study which does seem to indicate that average levels of scores have increased between generations was carried out by Tuddenham (1948). He compared the average scores of conscripts into the U.S. Army in World War I and World War II, administering the same intelligence test to the second world war recruits as had been used in 1917 with members of the earlier generation. On average, the World War II recruits scored at a level equivalent to two years of mental age higher than that of the World War I soldiers. Tuddenham interpreted this as reflecting the greater education of the second group of recruits, who had an average of Grade 10, whereas the first group's average education was Grade 8. Similarly, the studies carried out by Green (1969) and Miles and Miles (1932), which have already been referred to, strongly emphasized the role of education in fostering mental growth. Indeed, a number of classical studies of intellectual development have emphasized the importance of education and other kinds of environmental stimulation for the growth of intellect, including Wheeler's (1942) study of mountain children in Tennessee, and Gordon's (1923) study of canal boat and gypsy children in England. Stimulating agencies in the lives of younger generations such as Tuddenham's World War II recruits, which might explain their higher average scores, include not only education, but exposure to films and radio and, more recently, TV. More recent surveys such as that of Hunt (1961) also strongly implicate socio-economic and other environmental factors in the development of intelligence. Hunt's findings will be referred to more fully in a later section.

Without reviewing the extensive literature in this area in great detail, it can be said that there are strong grounds for believing that provision of a stimulating environment has very important effects on intellectual growth. The kinds of evidence available include studies of orphanage children who are or are not adopted, studies of identical and fraternal twins reared together and apart, studies of children of differing socio-economic status or race who have received special remedial treatment, studies of infants given special treatment, studies of brain development in rats, monkeys and cats, and so on. The evidence has, for example, led Bloom (1964) to conclude that

the growth of intelligence is heavily dependent upon "the environment in which individuals live and work" (p. 89). The
effects of the environment are apparently partly mediated by
improved nutrition, stimulated neuronal development and similar
physiological and biochemical factors. However, intellectual
growth is also affected by opportunities to acquire cognitive
skills, opportunities to acquire linguistic skills, development of motivational systems which foster determined effort in
the face of problems, development of confident attitudes which
mean that intellectual tasks are attacked with hope of success,
presence or absence of appropriate models of behaviour, and so
on. These kind of factors are most strongly developed in the
years up to the age of 10 (Bloom, 1976). Thus, experience in
a cognitive and socio-affective environment which fosters both
continuing development and a positive motivational and emotional climate for lifelong growth looks to be a major factor in
the course of intellectual/cognitive development. Lifelong education aims at providing such a climate.


## LEARNING OUTSIDE CONVENTIONAL SCHOOL AGES

While adults may carry out much less learning of the kind
seen in schoolchildren than do children of school age, the reason for this is not necessarily one of impaired capacity. For
example, it could also largely result from acceptance of the
view that school-like learning should only be done during the
conventional school years (Gelpi, 1976), along with rustiness
as a result of failure to exercise learning skills after adolescence. At this point, it is informative to ask whether people in real-life settings, actually do learn at ages other than
those at which schooling usually occurs. A related question,
although it will be dealt with in Chapter 5 and not here, is
that of whether learning in adults is carried on in ways similar to those in which it occurs among schoolchildren.


*Learning prior to school age*

There is very strong evidence that an enormous amount of
learning goes on in the pre-school years. Bloom (1964), for
example, concluded that fifty percent of mental development has
occurred by the age of 4. However, since most pre-school learning involves the acquisition of skills which adults and school-
age children take for granted, much of this learning goes un-
noticed. Due credit for the enormous learning task successfully carried out by most young children is seldom given. In

fact, by the age of 3-4 days, the newborn infant is already
responsive to stimulation. A certain degree of "skill" is
present from the first or second day (Kagan, Henker, Hen-Tov,
Levine and Lewis, 1966). There is even empirical evidence that
children actually learn prior to birth as is shown by studies
of conditioning foetal heart beat to an external stimulus like
the sound of a bell rung in the room in which the mother is
situated. Unborn infants can apparently also be conditioned to
changes in the maternal body chemistry. All this indicates
that the infant is by no means incompetent even in its very
early life (Kessen, 1967; Stone, Murphy and Smith, 1972).
    It is important to notice that this capacity of the very
young infant to interact and adapt to the external world ultimately serves as a basis for future development (e.g. Bruner,
1968). As the longitudinal studies of Bayley (1968) and others
have shown, even very early infancy is a period in which the
foundation learning on which all later life will rest takes
place. Consequently, the importance of this learning should
not be forgotten or disregarded because of the ease with which
the things the neonate learns are subsequently done by older
children and adults. What babies learn in the early months
and years affects the whole course of their life development.
    Among the learning tasks which are successfully negotiated
by most children at a very early age are the achievement of
depth perception (Walk and Gibson, 1961), the discrimination of
shapes and forms (Hebb, 1949), discrimination of patterns
(Fantz, 1963), discrimination of differing pitch (Leventhal and
Lipsitt, 1964), discrimination of different levels of loudness
(Bartoshuk, 1964), and so on. Within the first year of life,
not only are these sensory skills acquired, but major cognitive
and personal achievements are mastered including, for example,
object constancy (things still exist even when you cannot actually see them), the discrimination of self from environment
(Flavell, 1963), and the first use of symbolic behaviour
(Bruner, 1968).
    Communication with other people is learned in the first
few months (Vygotsky, 1962), and the basic foundations of language are laid in this period (Menyuk, 1971). With increasing
mastery of language, the subtleties of cause and effect are
learned, along with increasing capacity to understand the abstract world of the not here and not now, rather than depending
purely on the immediate physical environment (Bruner and Piaget
have both discussed this process in great detail). Early experience also appears to affect the development of perceptual
systems (e.g. Chow, Riesen and Newell, 1957), alertness and
interest in the external world (Sayegh and Dennis, 1965), vo-

cabulary and verbal skills (Burnett, Beach and Sullivan, 1963),
the ability to analyze and reflect upon the environment in abstract terms (Schubert and Cropley, 1972), and indeed the kinds
of basic skills which are closely correlated with subsequent
success in learning to read and doing well in school (e.g. Hunt,
1973).
     Many personality traits too are related to learning in
early childhood. The crucial bases of the capacity to relate
to other people are learned prior to the commencement of school
age (Erikson, 1968), as are the capacities to display appropriate mothering behaviours (Harlow, 1961), express hostility and
agression appropriately (Scott, 1958), seek success and achievement in school (e.g. Kagan and Moss, 1959), respond to different
kinds of reinforcement (Terrell, Durkin and Wiesley, 1955), be
curious and enquiring or avoid uncertainty (Berlyne, 1958), and
so on. Finally, the strategies or tactics through which children go about analyzing their experiences with the external
world are greatly influenced by learning carried out in the
first few years of life (e.g. Freeberg and Payne, 1967). Indeed, as Jencks (1972) has strikingly shown in a recent review
of the area, by the time they start school, children will cus-
tomarily not only have mastered the basics of the extremely
complex and abstract symbol systems constituted by their native
language, and have learned to coordinate their sense impres-
sions with the external world in a smooth and adaptive manner,
but they will have learned a whole complex of attitudes, feelings, motives and skills which recent evidence suggests are
scarcely modified by schooling.
     The evidence is, then, that learning prior to the com-
mencement of schooling is by no means a trivial matter. Not
only are basic survival and perceptual skills mastered, but
the elements of the cognitive skills which will be of major
importance in later life are already established in young children. Studies such as that of Jencks, which has just been
cited, attribute to very early learning an even more important
role in shaping the whole course of life than mere emphasis on
the major learning tasks which are mastered in early childhood
would suggest. In fact, Jencks has concluded, from an extensive analysis of data on factors modifying the school behaviour
of children in the U.S.A., that most of the variation from
child to child is caused by non-school factors. Paramount
among these are the attitudinal and motivational qualities acquired in the home. Major and crucial differences in these
areas are already well-established by the time school commences.
Thus, the importance of psychological development in the earliest years has a double base. On the one hand, intellectual

and cognitive development during that period provides a crucial
foundation for later development in those areas. On the other
hand, the motives and attitudes learned prior to the commencement of schooling set the whole pattern for the way in which
children will deploy their intellectual and cognitive skills in
later life. Since one major factor in the apparently diminished ability of adults to learn is their possession of negative attitudes and motivations towards learning, it is apparent
that, if learning is to be a lifelong affair, the pattern not
only of basic abilities, but also of attitudes and motives developed in early childhood will be an issue of crucial importance. This point emphasizes the importance of education during the earliest years.

*Learning beyond conventional school age*

　　As has already been shown, the conventional and traditional opinion is that people quickly deteriorate intellectually
beyond the age of 40 or so and that their learning capacity is
seriously impaired from about then (e.g. Comfort, 1964; Naylor
and Harwood, 1970). Citing Oesler and William James, McLeish
(1963, pp. 121-123) has pointed out that it is traditionally
accepted that the middle-aged and the old can learn little. One
result of this belief has been the great neglect of adults in
the study of learning. While it is true that this state of affairs has been partially corrected, since recent years have been
marked by an increased interest in the psychology of adults
(e.g. Bischoff, 1969; Bromley, 1974; Goulet and Baltes, 1970;
Neugarten, 1968), such studies have tended to concentrate on
the elderly, and have neglected people in the so-called "prime
of life" from about 30 to about 50 (Dubin, 1974). As a result,
the actual extent to which adults can learn is a subject largely settled by popular opinion and the misconception that people
beyond school years do not have the capacity or the inclination
to learn much.
　　This stereotype has been reinforced by conclusions such as
Lehman's (1953) that an overwhelming majority of creative people do their creative work before reaching their 40th birthdays.
He found that chemists reached their peak, generally-speaking,
between 26 and 30 years of age. Mathematicians peaked between
30 and 40, philosophers between 35 and 39. Authors did their
best work before reaching the age of 45, while movie actors
achieved their greatest popularity between 30 and 40. Of
course, many people in these fields did not conform to the
average cited; the figures given here are generalizations de-

scribing the overall picture as it was most frequently seen.
Nonetheless, although there are many known instances of creativity at early and late ages, Lehman concluded that creativity peaks in the 30s, and declines slowly thereafter. He
identified factors that he believed lead to decreased creativity with advancing age, and these factors have been extended by Bromley (1974, pp. 218-219). Some of them involve physical deterioration, as might have been expected. However, the
effect of acceptance of certain social roles inimical to creativity is also emphasized. For example, promotion, prestige
and leadership status may lead away from continued creative effort by channelling energy into administrative duties. There
may also be a tendency for many of those who achieve early creative success to rest on their laurels. On the other hand, inadequate recognition may destroy motivation to produce, as may
hostility from the young and upcoming, with subsequent social
pressure to be less active. Finally, Lehman drew attention to
the advantages of education and stimulation which have improved
across generations in recent history.

Thus, once again, although reduced creative achievement
may reflect diminished capacity, socio-affective variables seem
to be strongly implicated. The study of age and creativity
thus also suggests that an educational system which provides
positive motivation to continued productivity, social acceptance of new learning in adults, opportunities to change social
roles, confidence in oneself as a learner, and so on, would
greatly facilitate continued productivity and adaptability
throughout life.

In fact, there are strong grounds for disbelieving the
stereotype that adults do not and cannot learn. For example,
as has already been mentioned, adults clearly achieve enormous
amounts of social learning, to an extent that makes it clear
that they can and habitually do adapt and adjust to their environments (i.e. learn). Similarly, the findings concerning
creativity have been argued to be mainly an artefact of early
death among many of the creative subjects studied (Dennis,
1968). Obviously, those creative people who died young prod-
uced their creative solutions early in life, and just how creative they would have been had they lived longer is not known.

Findings about the ability of adults to learn in areas
other than social development and reflective or creative thinking also exist. A number of studies have shown that people
well beyond school age are perfectly capable of mastering a
wide variety of tasks, some of them very like the kinds of
thing that schoolchildren master. Earlier sections have reported that adult abilities are highest in verbal areas, and

relevant literature supports this expectation.  Studies by, for
example, Thorndike (in McLeish, 1963) in which elderly people
learned Esperanto, and Cheydleur (in McLeish, 1963) in which
they learned French, are consistent with this expectation.
Naylor and Harwood (1970) confirmed the more rapid fall-off on
the sensory and motor tasks of an adult intelligence scale (the
WAIS) among elderly people, but they also demonstrated· that
they still showed high levels of ability on certain school-like
tasks.  When translation from German to English was taught to
elderly people, it was found that about half of them achieved
a German-English translation level equivalent to university
entrance standard in only 6 months of instruction.  One of the
best students was 88.

Nor is learning among adults confined to verbal skills.
In the U.S.A. for example, the Federal Aeronautics Authority
permitted commercial airline pilots up to age 55 to attempt to
convert from piston-engine aircraft to jets, when the latter
kind of aircraft began to predominate.  Despite the belief that
mastering a psychomotor task at this level of difficulty would
be impossible for pilots beyond about 40, McFarland and O'Dough-
erty (1959) reported that results indicated that pilots up to
about age 60 could still acquire the new skills required for
flying jets, and continue as efficient pilots.  In fact, as
Tough (1971) has shown, adults continually seek further learning although not necessarily in settings reminiscent of the
conventional class room.  They voluntarily undertake study in
a wide range of areas, from clinical psychology and child development to business management and ecology.  He reported that
an average North American adult spends no less than 700 hours
a year in learning projects of that kind.

Dubin (1974) pointed out that increasingly large numbers
of adults who have established themselves in a first career are
subsequently seeking to learn a new one later in life.  Johnstone and Rivera (1965) coined the apt phrase "volunteers for
learning" to describe the large number of adults seeking further education, usually through adult-education facilities.
According to these authors most Americans seeking adult education are between 25 and 45 years of age, while they tend to be
relatively well-educated already, and of middle-class socio-
economic status.  Similar findings have been reported by Knox
(1965) and London (1964).

Learning late in life is becoming something much more than
a matter of job-advancement, pursuit of a hobby, or a way of
passing time.  For increasingly large numbers of adults, continued learning beyond school age has become not a fad or a
recreation, but a necessity.  Many of them face the possibility

of becoming obsolete unless they can adjust and adapt to change.
This important aspect of continued learning among adults has
been discussed in detail by Dubin (1974). He has utilized the
concept of "half-life" as a way of understanding the role of
continued learning in already-skilled adults. The half-life of
a skill is the number of years after which trained people are
only half as competent as they were on completion of initial
training. Dubin cites estimates that the half-life of a recent
engineering graduate is five years, and that of a present-day
engineering course a similar period of time. By contrast, the
half-life of new engineers about 25 years ago was a matter of
12 years, so that the period needed to become only 50 percent
competent is decreasing. For doctors specializing in internal
medicine, he cites a half-life of 3 years. Thus, continued
learning beyond school age is not only something which lies
within the capacity of adults, but something which is becoming
a necessity for them.


*Factors inhibiting continued learning in adults*

It is pertinent to ask, at this point, what factors inhibit continued learning in adults. According to Dubin (1974),
one important element of the problem involves institutional
factors. Trained specialists tend to gravitate to positions as
administrators as they get older, rather than remaining practitioners. They are removed from actual contact with the day-to-
day practice of their profession, and have their time consumed
by administrative and interpersonal issues. As a result of
this institutional position as an administrator rather than a
practitioner, they are remote from the sources of updating, and
may even find themselves in charge of juniors who are better
prepared in a basic skills and knowledge than they themselves
are. This problem clearly implies that part of continued learning for highly-trained individuals will involve re-examination
of relationships between workers and work-organizations, and
among workers themselves.
Dubin also draws attention to the effects of a second inhibiting factor. Excessive specialization may reduce adults'
ability to adjust to change. On the one hand, narrow specialization results in a commitment to a discipline so restricted
in content that a slight shift in the requirements of the profession renders the specialist's skills obsolete. On the other
hand, the position is compounded by the problem that excessive
specialization makes later learning difficult. For example,
it provides knowledge-getting skills that do not lend them-

selves readily to transfer to other areas, while the over-spe-
cialist also has a poor base of general principles and concepts onto which to build the details of later, new learning.
One implication of this view is that the ability to adjust to
changed circumstances will be enhanced by earlier training in
broad principles and the inter-relationships among data.

However, in addition to such institutional factors which
inhibit continued learning in adults, it is necessary to recognize the importance of financial, cultural and psychological
barriers (Gelpi, 1976). For example, the organization of work
and the development of an individual's vocational career involve decreasing emphasis on acquiring new knowledge and skills
and the expectation, as middle age and older age ensue, of a
process of decreasing financial security, decreasing influence,
and decreasing ability to influence the course of events. The
society expects people to become out of date as they become
older, and to play a more and more passive role. They are expected to become fixed in their ways, and passively to accept
a decreasing say in even their own lives. With increasing age
individuals become increasingly aware that they are obsolete
and powerless. It is small wonder that many of them accept
that the basic cause of their alienation is change and novelty,
and come to regard the new with suspicion and hostility. As a
result, many adults accept and even endorse the notion that
adulthood is a time of steadily decreasing ability to learn,
and they may even feel hostile or fearful towards the new.

What is needed in view of this state of affairs has been
described by Gelpi (1976, p. 191) as "une politique de troisième âge" in which adults, and especially the elderly, will be
permitted by the organization of society to play an active role
in the planning and control of their own lives, and to carry
out whatever learning this necessitates. The intrapsychic property needed to put such a set of societal values into effect
has been described by Dubin (1974) as "personal initiative".
Some people are not only able to learn, but are ready and willing to do so. By contrast, others apparently accept the stereotype that learning ends when schooling ends. In other words,
an important factor influencing enduring readiness to learn is
the existence of financial and social structures which permit
or even encourage it, along with appropriate attitudes towards
oneself as a learner and towards new knowledge as a goal. Again,
then, it is apparent that learning in the sense of continuing
adaptation to changing circumstances, is a complex not only of
appropriate cognitive factors (possession of transferable
skills, understanding of the inter-relatedness of elements of
knowledge, and so on), but also of motivational and attitudinal

factors, both within the society and within the individual.

## IMPLICATIONS FOR THE CONCEPT OF LIFELONG EDUCATION

The primary purpose of the present chapter has been to ask whether one of the major basic psychological assumptions made by proponents of lifelong education, namely that people are capable of learning (in the broad sense defined earlier) at ages other than those conventionally spent in school, is reasonable in the light of current psychological knowledge. As has been seen, a review of the literature suggests that, despite the prevailing stereotypes to the contrary, intellect continues to function vigorously in early adulthood, middle age and even old age, that children of pre-school age are capable of learning, and that the learning which occurs prior to school age is of a vital importance to the entire course of life. The basic premises of lifelong education in the area thus appear to be well-founded. Indeed, it would not be unreasonable to say that the importance of very early learning is so great as to suggest that any prudent society would be well-advised to make formal provision for the needs of pre-school children. Evidence concerning technological, socio-political, vocational and economic change-processes which are currently in train also suggests that recognition of the continuing adjustment capacities of adults would also be, to say the very least, appropriate on the part of educational planners.

Since, however, fostering of learning includes not only provision of appropriate cognitive material, but also establishment of a learning-facilitating environment, the key elements of which are the attitudes and motivations of potential learners, a formal system of lifelong education will need to be structured, not only in terms of the cognitive needs of the people involved in the system, but also in terms of their motivational and socio-effective needs. Those who *will not*, or *fear to* learn are as handicapped as they would be if they really *could not*.

# Chapter 5

# The Vertical Integration of
# Intellectual Functioning

## COGNITIVE FUNCTIONING AND AGE

*Styles of intellectual functioning*

The term "cognition" or "cognitive processes" is used in a
variety of ways in psychological writings. Frequently, it is
difficult to see where the concept of intelligence ends, and
that of cognition begins. In general, the term "cognition" is
used to refer to a set of psychological processes through which
people interpret, store, and subsequently re-apply information
they receive from their environments. Thus, cognitive theories
are usually heavily bound up with concepts like that of "information," "meaning," "awareness," and so on. In a nutshell,
cognitive theorists conceptualize a human being as an organized,
autonomous system of skills, knowledge, motivations and emotions that is in a state of continual interaction with the external world. Any discrepancy between the system's "map" or
"model" and the external world can be said to contain information or to have meaning. Sometimes the term "surprise" or a
similar notion is used to refer to this state of awareness of
a mis-match between internal representations and the external
environment.

When people become aware of a mis-match (i.e. they are
"surprised" by the environment, and so receive information from
it), it is necessary for them to interpret the new stimulus
(i.e., to work out its meaning). This process of interpretation is sometimes referred to as "decoding" of incoming information. What we usually call "meaning" is thus only partly
determined by the objective properties of a perceived stimulus.
It also depends on how the stimulus is "decoded" by the person
who perceives it. In other words, experiences actually have
meaning *assigned* to them by the persons undergoing them. This
is not to say that meaning is unrelated to the objective prop-

erties of a stimulus.  On the contrary, the process of decoding
or assignment of meaning involves matching up the properties of
a new stimulus with existing information about what states normally co-exist.  A new stimulus is assigned to membership in a
group of other events experienced on earlier occasions, with
which it has key attributes in common.  These existing sets of
closely related prior experiences are often called "categories".
        A category, then, is a set of stored information about
what environmental events go together. It will normally specify
the criterion characteristics necessary for a new experience to
be coded as a member of the category.  It will also usually contain information about what kinds of behaviours are appropriate
to members of the category.  For example, a spherical reddish
object of about tennis-ball size, with a shiny skin and a short
stalk projecting from one of its slightly flattened surfaces,
may readily be interpreted (coded) as a member of the category
"apple".  This interpretation will, in turn, imply that eating
is an appropriate behaviour towards the new stimulus.  It is
worth noting at this point that categories may themselves be
linked into broader categories such as that of "fruit".
        This model of human psychological functioning implies that
it is an active or interactive process, in which understanding
of what is going on around a person is partly dependent on previous experience with the world.  It also implies that "reality"
is, to some extent, in the eye of the beholder, and that meaning is assigned to events rather than being inherent in them.
For example, miscoding of experiences is perfectly possible.
This could occur when a particular category was unusually readily available, so that a stimulus which did not really fit well
could be inappropriately coded into it.  The result may be behaviour quite inappropriate to the "real" nature of the stimulus.  For example, a hungry person might readily decode small,
spherical, red objects growing on a bush as "food", regardless
of their edibility.  Basically then cognitive processes involve
coordination of present experiences to a kind of map or model
of reality which has been built up as a result of past experiences.  The process is subject to distortion and error, and, as
will be shown more fully in following paragraphs, is also idiosyncratic.
        The contrast with the concept of intelligence is still not
completely clear.  Many people would probably say that the processes just described correspond quite closely to what they mean
when they use the word "intelligence".  Nonetheless, it is possible to see the elements of a clear distinction at this point.
Intelligence is more conventionally employed to refer to the
speed and accuracy of recognition and recall of stimuli, the

breadth of the range of information that can be simultaneously
held in attention, the accuracy with which previously-learned
data can be reproduced, the state of general alertness, and so
on. To some extent, then, the kinds of processes referred to
by the term "intelligence" are the capacities, skills, strategies, and degree of efficiency with which the constituent steps
of cognition are carried out. Intelligence can, therefore, be
seen as part of cognition, a sub-set of the cognitive processes,
as it were, or one of the tools through which cognitive processes are carried out.

A second major distinction which supplements the one just
made is that it is customary to think of intelligence in terms
of relative presence or relative absence. Intelligence, then,
is essentially a quantitative concept. Discussion of intelligence, as in Chapter 4, conventionally centres around the extent to which such-and-such an ability is more present or less
present. By contrast, cognition is essentially a qualitative
concept referring to the tactics or strategies which people
employ in making sense out of their experience. Cognitive theorists are more concerned with the patterns or styles through
which interpretation of the world is carried out. This also
means that statements about differences in cognitive functioning are far less often evaluative than are statements about
intelligence. Throughout the present text the key distinction
which will be made between concepts of intelligence and cognitive functioning will centre on this difference -- discussions
of intelligence and age will be concerned with differences in
level, efficiency or power of various age groups in carrying
out certain kinds of tasks. Statements about cognitive processes will refer to differences in the styles or patterns
through which knowledge and experience are co-ordinated.


*Differentiation of abilities*

Although it has just been suggested that intelligence is
essentially a quantitative concept which concerns itself with
levels rather than patterns of intellectual functioning, traditional studies of intelligence include some conceptualizations
which give greater emphasis to qualitative than to quantitative
factors. This is particularly apparent in studies which emphasize, not levels of ability, but kinds of ability. In fact,
such studies provide a link between the concept of intelligence
and that of cognitive functioning. As will become apparent
later, examination of kinds of intelligence rather than levels
of intelligence lends itself particularly well to the analysis

of the relationship between age and psychological function. Essentially, qualitative analysis of intelligence involves treating its growth as at least partly a matter of changes in the relative importance of certain kinds of ability, and of changes in the patterns of abilities that are brought to bear on intellectual tasks. Intelligence can then be conceptualized as involving the development of characteristic styles of intellectual functioning in different people.

This conceptualization of intellectual development is by no means new. Garrett (e.g., Garrett, 1946) proposed a developmental theory of intellectual organization, according to which increasing age is accompanied by a shift from dependence upon the application of a single amorphous general ability to all intellectual tasks, to the increasing utilization of specialized abilities acquired during the process of psychological development. This phenomenon of increasing utilization of narrow, special abilities, and decreasing use of a broad, amorphous highly generalized intelligence was labelled by Garrett "differentiation of abilities". The concept has also been applied in the study of English children by Burt (1954). He concluded that differentiation of abilities is a natural process which occurs with increasing age.

However, there is no universal agreement on the question of whether differentiation of abilities is an inherent feature of intellectual development. Some studies, (e.g., Cropley, 1964) have reported that the opposite effect (integration of abilities) occurs in some children between certain ages. The apparent discrepancy between these kinds of finding has been resolved by Vernon (1950). He concluded that differentiation of abilities is not an inherent process, but that it is highly dependent upon the kinds of environmental stimulation a child receives. The organization of education is apparently a key factor in fostering or inhibiting differentiation of abilities. Dockrell (1963) for example, showed that English school-children in the early years at Grammar school displayed much more advanced differentiation of abilities than children from secondary modern schools. Thus, there are grounds for believing that the environment, and especially schooling, plays an important role in determining whether intelligence becomes increasingly more differentiated (specialized) with advancing age, or whether the tendency to depend heavily on a highly-generalized skill persists.

*"Fluid" versus "crystallized" intelligence*

A second major qualitative theory in the area of intellec-

tual development is that of "fluid" and "crystallized" intelligence (see Horn 1968). According to this formulation, intelligence in the young is general, formless, and highly plastic
(i.e. it is "fluid"). With intellectual development, special
abilities are formed in response to environmental stimulation
(i.e. they "crystallize" out from the formless but plastic fluid intelligence). An increasing proportion of crystallized
intelligence results in decreasing availability of crystalli-
zable, fluid intelligence. One result of this is a decrease in
flexibility among the elderly, because most of their fluid intelligence has already been crystallized during their lives.
This means, among other things, that a test concentrating on
fluid intelligence would indicate an apparent fall-off in intelligence among older subjects, whereas a test emphasizing
crystallized intelligence (such as vocabulary) would tend to
favour older people.

Thus, a second explanation of the apparent decline in intellectual power with increasing age lies in the argument that
the pattern or style of intelligence changes with increasing
age. Hofstaetter (1954) and Smart (1965) have analyzed intelligence tests and concluded that the tests measure quite different abilities at differing ages. Although their methods of
data analysis have been severely criticized by Cronbach (1967),
the notion of a change in the style of intelligence with increasing age is a persuasive one, with implications both for
the understanding of relationships between intelligence and
age, and also for the design of schooling. For example, it
suggests that the saying "You can't teach an old dog new tricks"
would be correct if it were worded as follows: "You can't
teach an old dog the tricks it could have learned when it was
a puppy, unless you teach them in ways that are suitable to an
old dog's intelligence."

Recognition of the role of schooling in facilitating or
inhibiting differentiation of abilities is paralleled by writers concerned with fluid and crystallized intelligence. Although they regard fluid intelligence as essentially a bio-
logically-based phenomenon, they acknowledge that the development of crystallized intelligence is greatly affected by the
environment. Although the simile is perhaps over-simplified,
the relationship of crystallized intelligence to environment
looks to be somewhat similar to the relationship between the
form of a jelly and the moulds which the cook employs. The
jelly is the same jelly and the same volume is used whether a
pint of liquid jelly is poured into an ordinary bowl or into
a fancy shape, say that of a rabbit. However, the form of the
result is quite different, and the kinds of situation for which

the two jellies are suitable are quite different; ask a small
child having a birthday party whether he would prefer the ordinary shape or the rabbit. The key idea for lifelong education is that the pattern or style of intelligence may be different at differing age levels suggesting, in turn, that the
nature of schooling at different ages should be related to this
phenomenon.

## STYLE OF COGNITIVE FUNCTIONING

*Cognitive styles*

The cognitive processes involve systematic interpretation
and reorganization of the information that is received as a result of interaction with the environment. Cognition encompas-
ses organization of memory, selection of key elements of stimuli, interpretation of experience through the process of coding,
and so on. It is not merely a phenomenon of visual perception
(e.g. Witkin, in Scheerer, 1964), but transcends mere sensory
reception of information. Cognitive processes involve a comprehensive organization of internal information-processing systems. However, just as it is possible to discern differences
in the ways in which different people deploy their intelligence,
it is possible to observe systematic and idiosyncratic, qualitative differences between individual people in the way in
which they carry out the organizing processes referred to here
as "cognition".
For example, some individuals, when asked to recall previously-learned material, regularly "fill in" gaps in their recall with explicatory material (Paul, 1954). Others (Klein,
1970) simply recall the basic, "factual" skeleton, stripping
away all more-or-less superfluous details. Klein refers to
this qualitative dimension of individual differences in cognitive processes as "importing" versus "skeletonizing". Some
people minimize variations in different elements of stimulus
material, hardly noticing minor differences of detail. Others
emphasize and even exaggerate such minor differences. Klein
(1951) referred to "levelling" versus "sharpening" in describ-
ing this dimension of individual difference. A third dimension
of cognitive style concerns the tendency of some people to attend to a very broad range of environmental stimuli, and to try
to co-ordinate them into a broad, generalized whole. Others
concentrate on a narrow subset of a complex stimulus and interpret it in terms of this restricted sampling. This difference
is referred to by Klein (1970) as "focussing" versus "scanning".
Other related kinds of qualitative difference are, for

example, differing degrees of tolerance of ambiguity and uncertainty, and differing preference for complexity as against
simplicity (e.g. Schroder, Driver and Streufert, 1967). The
important point for the present purposes is that people differ
systematically and consistently in the kinds of interaction
with the environment they prefer, and in the kinds of information they extract from environmental experience. Some attend
to a very broad range of events, distinguish sharply between
relatively similar pieces of information, inter-relate such
information into very broad concepts, and so on, whereas others
may focus on a very narrow span of information, bring into
close attention a few key features of the information, and form
a large number of very narrow and finely-discriminated concepts.
A great variety of "styles" is possible, even if cognitive
function were fully described by the three dimensions of importing versus skeletonizing, levelling versus sharpening, and
focussing versus scanning. In fact, the relevant literature
identifies more dimensions than these, but as the present purpose is merely to acquaint the reader with the broad concept,
a certain "coding" of the material involving scanning, levelling and skeletonizing has been carried out.

*Cognitive styles and the teacher*

Two major points are of relevance here. The first point
(to be developed more fully in following sections) concerns the
fact that styles of cognitive functioning are apparently modified by, for example, successes or failures in coping with experience. Where a particular style has been "successful", future adoption of that particular pattern of functioning is encouraged, and vice versa. Thus, whether a child acquires a
broad set of cognitive tactics for interpreting and relating
to his environment, or some other style of functioning, is
partly dependent upon the kinds of "practice" he experiences.
In the classroom setting, this suggests that the child who is
punished for unorthodoxy will learn to avoid the unfamiliar,
to resist change, and to focus his attention on minor details
of his environment which signal to him that his behaviour is
"right" or "wrong". There are ground for believing that such
tendencies persist throughout life. Cropley and Sikand (1973)
have suggested that one major feature of the difference in cognitive functioning between highly creative people and schizo-
phrenic patients lies in the ability of the creatives to tolerate perception of incongruity and uncertainty in their environments without excessive anxiety.

The amenability of cognitive styles to training is of very
great importance for lifelong education.  Continued readiness
to adapt to changing environmental demands and to utilize further learning as a coping technique involves the willingness of
adults to continue to learn, their ability to tolerate anxiety
arising from re-assuming the role of learner, and so on.  This
point has already been developed in some detail in Chapter 4.
At the age level which currently constitutes the pre-school
years, the importance of experience for subsequent cognitive
style has been emphasized by, for example, Freeberg and Payne
(1967).  Thus, the way in which people adjust to the kinds of
later-life changes that have been outlined in Chapter 2 is
closely related to the styles of cognitive functioning they
have developed in earlier years.  Furthermore, a great deal of
the learning involved in cognitive development occurs in very
early years.  This means that pre-school education, education
during the conventional school years, and learning later in
life are all closely inter-related through the phenomena of
cognitive development.  Again, then, the unity of education as
a lifelong process is emphasized.

## THE COURSE OF COGNITIVE GROWTH

It has already been argued that cognitive development dif-
fers from person to person, and that it is modified by experience.  Moreover, the whole process of cognitive development is
highly interactive, in that pre-existing systems for processing
information (themselves largely the result of experience) modify the ways in which later experience will be perceived and
interpreted, and thus modify cognitive growth.  This means that
cognitive growth experiences in the past, present and future
are all closely inter-related, being both a result of, and also
determiners of each other.
Although writers differ concerning the extent to which the
capacity to make sense out of the environment is innate, there
is general agreement that it develops as a result of experience.
As James (1890) put it, the external world of a new-born infant
must be a "blooming, buzzing confusion", but as a result of cognitive growth, the recurrent regularities of what is at first a
collection of unrelated events are noticed, and eventually a
stable framework is imposed on experience.  A person comes, for
example, to recognize that events are organized and patterned,
that some of them are more or less equivalent to each other,
and that the occurrence of certain events is a signal for the
probable occurrence of others.  Cognitive growth thus involves

development of the ability to impose some sort of order on experience, and in doing so to render it meaningful.  A number
of writers have described the course of this growth in various
ways.  Three major conceptualizations will be described in the
following sections.

*Piaget and the development of intelligence*

Probably the most widely known of writers on cognitive development is Piaget.  Although a detailed account of his developmental psychology is beyond the scope of the present chapter,
it is worthwhile to sketch out its main features.  According to
Piaget, there are basically four major stages of cognitive
growth, ranging from the earliest kind of function seen in the
tiny infant, to that characteristic of the mature adult.  In
the first broad stage, which he calls the *sensori-motor period*
(Phillips, 1969), Piaget emphasizes the fact that small children are bound to immediate, concrete events which impinge upon
their sensory apparatus, and that their responses are limited
to motor reactions to such sensory inputs.  At best, an infant
at this stage can develop the ability to emit anticipatory reactions to concrete events shortly before their actual occurrence.

During the second broad stage, *the pre-operational stage*
(Phillips, 1969), objects are seen to exist even when they are
not impinging on sensory systems.  Anticipations and expectations transcend the merely immediate and concrete, the concept
of cause and effect emerges (although initially in a very rudimentary form), and late in the stage, language appears as a new
principle for imposing order and structure on the environment.
In the third stage, that of *concrete operations*, the individual
comes to be able to carry out "operations" on the environment.
Children develop an ability to disentangle cause and effect, to
form hypotheses about likely consequences of certain actions,
to grasp something of the organization of events which render
the external world coherent and to co-ordinate their own behaviour in terms of that understanding.  However, insight into
the "facts" of the world around them is still derived from
their own, personal, concrete experience, and is couched mainly
in terms of real-life concrete causes and effects (hence "concrete" operations).

The final stage of cognitive development is that of *formal
operations*.  In this stage, the abstract principles out of
which the concrete facts arise are grasped.  This means that
events can be understood in terms of their symbolic "meaning".

Theoretical possibilities can be weighed without the necessity
for them actually to take place, and behaviour can be attuned
to theoretical possibilities that may never happen. The formal
operator, in fact, comes to be able to deal with the world in
terms of abstract, symbolic generalizations. At this stage,
people can learn without direct experience, and can respond to
abstract propositions. A major result of this development is
that the individual is freed from dependence upon the immediate
sensory environment for concrete cues, and can behave with a
stability and consistency transcending the relative instability
of immediate sensory events.

According to Piaget, the order of these four stages is in-
variant. The basic mechanism which permits development to occur is twofold, involving the capacity to relate new experience
to existing cognitive structures on the one hand (assimilation),
and the capacity to adapt existing structures to mis-matches
with environmental inputs, on the other (accommodation). The
stages are not discrete, but overlapping, since a predominance
of cognitive functioning characteristic of one stage does not
preclude the occurrence of functioning characteristic of an
earlier stage. In fact, cognition in a given person is likely
to involve a mixture of stages, according to how thoroughly the
highest stage reached has been mastered. Piaget sees the process as basically biological in nature, with environment making
little difference, provided that minimum levels of disagreement
between existing structures and new information are provided.
For differing societies it is possible to define approximate
age levels within which the various stages merge into one another. Nonetheless, not all people progress into the formal
operations stage, regardless of their age, while for many, formal operational thinking frequently breaks down, for example
under pressure or emotional strain. Thus, Piaget's developmental psychology allows for the existence of a wide variety
of inter-personal differences in cognitive function, according
to the particular patterns of interaction between different
individuals and their environments. Again, despite the apparently heavily biological orientation of Piaget's formulations,
a role is assigned for education, in the sense that different
degrees of cognitive development and different levels of ability to sustain higher-level cognitive functioning under, for
example, stressful conditions, would apparently result from
different patterns of experience.

*Vygotsky's emphasis on the role of language*
Although Piaget described language as a key element in

formal operational thinking, and saw the emergence of language
as a crucial step in cognitive development, the inter-relationship of thought and language has been most explicitly stated by
Vygotsky (1962). Following a conceptualization which has subsequently been further developed by Luria (1961), he argued
that the development of intelligence and the development of
language are closely-linked. The influence of speech on intelligence is profound, and it is speech which permits the extensive development of cognitive processes seen in man. Nonetheless, according to Vygotsky, language and thought have separate
roots and are originally independent. In its earliest forms,
language is public (cries, grunts, exclamations and the like),
and serves an emotional and rudimentary social function. Just
as there is much "thoughtless language", there is also "lan-
guageless thought", as is seen in, say, the rudimentary use of
simple tools by primates to solve problems (Köhler's apes are
an example).

It is only when language becomes internalized, when it
becomes a tool of internal processes rather than an emotional
releaser (as in, say, a cry of rage), or a social signal (as in,
say, crooning by a baby or the purring of a cat, which signify
contentment), that true thought occurs. This process is uni-
quely human, and permits a new basis for relations with the external world that is impossible without the use of some complex
abstract system of signals. Vygotsky points out that language
per se is not strictly necessary for true thought, but that
some symbolic signal system of equivalent complexity and flexibility is necessary. Language is certainly the best known
such system.

The first stage of cognitive growth described by Vygotsky
is that of *syncretic thinking*. This kind of thought is pre-
linguistic, pre-logical, concrete and labile. The "true" relationships between events are not noticed, and events which
are spatially or temporally contiguous are thought to belong
together. Human and infra-human thought have much in common at
this level. The second level of cognitive development involves
what Vygotsky called *complexive thinking*. This kind of thinking requires the use of language as a representational system
that provides labels for concrete events in the external environment. Perceived relationships among experiences begin to
involve the "true" basis, and the individual is no longer confined to lumping together events which happen to occur close
to each other either in time or in physical space. However,
the connections among events are still dominated by either
their concrete properties or by relationships which, while lin-
guistically possible, are not implied by strict logic and miss

the essential principles involved.  For example, a complexive
thinker might say that an umbrella and chewing gum are similar
because, if it were raining, one could either go outside with
the protection of an umbrella, or else stay at home and chew
gum.
     It is only when language and thought merge that a new kind
of thought, *verbal thought*, emerges.  At this time cognitive
processes are transformed, since for people capable of verbal
thought, a new way of interacting with the external world
exists.  Verbal thinkers can speculate about what the world
would be like if certain conditions ever came into existence
even though these conditions have never previously been known,
so that they can invent and create.  They are also able to
learn about things they have never themselves experienced by
learning from the verbalizations of others, whereas the very
young are confined in their acquisition of wisdom to concrete
experience with the present environment.
     The instrument which makes it possible for parents, and
subsequently the other educative agencies in a society, to
transmit knowledge abstractly is language. Those who teach children tell them what goes with what, what is the safest way to
behave towards such and such an event, and so on.  Because of
its abstractness, language makes it possible to link events
which are far apart in time and physical space, and permits
generalized thinking about classes of events.  For example, to
label a bottle a weapon is to transform the "meaning" of the object and to "tune-up" a whole new class of information about
it.  Through language, then, educative agencies transform children's environments, providing knowledge far beyond what they
could acquire purely on the basis of a lifetime of actual experience, and provide a ready-make pattern or model, in terms
of which to interpret and understand the external world.
     Both scholarly study and common experience indicate that,
although these interpretative frameworks differ from person to
person in a given society, they are sufficiently homogenized
within a society to permit the description of national stereotypes or national "modal personalities" (e.g. McDavid and
Harari, 1968).  Through the process of socialization, people
are taught a relatively standardized set of beliefs about the
nature of the world.  For present purposes, this phenomenon of
educative shaping of the *Weltanschauung* of children is of considerable interest.  It emphasizes the capacity of a society
and its educative agencies (family, friendship groups, school,
and so on) to modify people's notions of how the world is structured, who and what they themselves are, what is appropriate
and inappropriate behaviour, and so on, without the precepts

being subjected to the empirical test of actual experience. Cognitive development at the level seen in human beings has, therefore, great potential for individuality, but it also has great
potential for conformity and stereotypy.

*Bruner and the building of one's own "reality"*

    The key concepts in Bruner's (1957, 1964) theory of cog-
nitive development are those of "coding" and "representation".
The process of representation is that through which events occurring in the external world are represented within a human
observer, the process through which real-life events are mir-
rored or represented "inside the skin", as it were. Since the
momentary fluctuations and minor inconsistencies in events are
too complex and unstable to be recorded and responded to separately as distinct events, cognition must involve a process of
selection of the recurrent regularities of experience and group-
ing of bits of information which constitute, for all practical
purposes, the same event or exemplars of the same class of
events, differing only in incidental details and in time and
place. What happens, according to Bruner, is that classes of
functionally equivalent happenings are identified, and new
events are given meaning, by being classified as members of
such and such a class of events. A class is referred to as a
"category", and the process of identifying the category into
which an instance fits is called "coding". Representation,
then, is a matter of coding environmental stimuli into categories. Where such coding is inappropriate (or as Bruner calls
it, "non-veridical"), the representation of what is happening
that is obtained will be distorted, and the interpretation of
events will differ from "reality".
    In fact, of course, the question of just what is "reality"
is a difficult one, since each person can be said to build his
own reality through the process of coding. In fact, this is a
key idea in Bruner's cognitive psychology: in a sense individuals construct the world in which they live, since "meaning"
results from coding, and coding is based on an individual's
own learned system of categories. The accessibility of categories is also subject to short-term fluctuations, for example
through recent experience with a particular category which
makes it unusually accessible (i.e. a person who has just been
eating might be particularly ready to code something lying on
a table as food and, perhaps, to attempt to eat a piece of wax
fruit). This phenomenon corresponds to what is called "set"
in other theoretical systems. Similarly, unusual emotional

turmoil might effect the accessibility of certain categories,
so that an angry person might mis-code as a physical assault
a friendly slap on the back from a friend.  Again, the "incorrect" coding would lead to behaviour perfectly consistent
with the "reality" constructed by the recipient of the slap,
(who might, for example, turn and punch the slapper), but quite
inappropriate to the "reality" of the person delivering the
slap (who might anticipate, say, a handshake).  The process of
co-ordinating external information, internal representations
of that information, and eventual behaviour, is called "integration" by Bruner.

    According to Bruner's developmental psychology, there are
three modes by which the recurrent regularities of experience
are internalized (i.e. through which experience is coded and
represented).  These modes form a temporal sequence during the
course of cognitive development.  The first, which characterizes young children, involves coding through actual motor movements, of what Bruner (e.g. 1964, p. 2) calls "enactive representation".  In the stage of enactive representation, the external world is coded according to actual motor movements which
are appropriate.  For example small children, when asked to say
what a comb is, may respond by making movements of their hands
and arms which approximate the movements needed for combing
the hair.  They store information about a comb by recording the
motor movements implied by a comb.  Storage is, as it were "in
the muscles".  Such coding requires, of course, actual experience in motor manipulation of stimuli, and is extremely inflex-
ible and difficult to communicate.

    The second stage in what Bruner (1964) calls "the growth
of mind" or "a series of technological advances in the use of
mind" involves representation through internal images.  Bruner
labels this "ikonic representation".  The internal images bear
an exact relationship to what is being represented in the same
way as a photograph bears a one-to-one relationship to what was
photographed.  Thus, although ikonic encoding represents a considerable advance over enactive encoding in terms of its remov-
al from strict dependence on actual, concrete, physical actions,
and has a certain degree of abstractness, it is still dependent
upon actual contact with whatever is being represented, and is
rigidly fixed to a specific object, as a photograph is linked
to the thing it is a photograph of.

    The third level of representation is eventually added to
the two lower levels with the acquisition of language and the
consequent emergence of the ability to code experience symbol-
ically.  With language comes a tool for extracting from concrete experience the key general properties, and the subsequent

inter-relationship of new experience with earlier experiences
to which it is logically related. At this stage of cognitive
development, the individual is, to a great extent, freed from
the tyranny of the immediate sensory environment (Bruner and
Olver, 1963). Experience can be dealt with in general and abstract terms, ideas are readily transmissable through verbal
communication, and so on.
    Clearly, a central concept in this formulation is the role
assigned to language. The key properties that Bruner discerns
in language are that it is "arbitrary" and "remote". What he
is referring to is the fact that verbal labels are independent
of the objects and relationships to which they refer. This
means that concepts can simultaneously have great stability
(regardless of momentary fluctuations in the concrete environment), and also great flexibility (since modification of a lan-
guage-coded concept is merely a matter of manipulation of the
abstractions contained in the words, and does not require actual transformation of tangible reality). One result of this
state of affairs is that speculation and hypothesis are possible.
    It should be noted that achievement of symbolic encoding
does not mean that earlier forms of representation disappear.
On the contrary, more cognitively mature individuals continue to
be capable of encoding according to earlier principles. Indeed, it seems likely that they will do so under certain affective conditions (e.g. when they are afraid or excited). Furthermore, Bruner's developmental psychology seems to imply that
a person could be skilful at symbolic encoding of scientific
information, as a result of his training in this area, but more
inclined to encode ikonically when trying to mend a TV set.
Again, it seems that people may be expected to differ in the
extent to which symbolic encoding is easy, habitual and fluent,
with one person trained to represent experience abstractly and
flexibly, another having developed a preference for ikonic or
even enactive encoding.

## IMPLICATIONS FOR LIFELONG EDUCATION

*Vertical integration of development*

    The present review of the psychological literature indi-
cates that cognitive growth is a highly interlocking process.
Each step or stage is connected to earlier stages in that it
arises out of them. On the other hand, it is also connected
to later stages, in that it provides a basis for them. Growth
is, in fact, integrated over time, or *vertically integrated*.

D

This interlocking growth process begins in earliest infancy so
that it is lifelong.  In short, then, learning is rightly viewed as a continuous fabric stretching over a lifetime.  Furthermore, it is dependent upon experience.  Meaning is something
which, to a certain extent, each person constructs for himself.
Understanding of the nature of the world is acquired as a result of experience with it, but is modified by social conventions, vicarious knowledge transmitted through other people's
verbalizations, and so on.  In other words, cognitive growth is
a complex, inter-connected learning process that is lifelong
and is modified by the kind of environment experienced from
earliest childhood.  This psychological analysis of cognitive
growth offers considerable support for the basic concepts of
lifelong education.


*Implications for classroom organization*

A second feature of the analysis of cognitive growth is
its implications for the way in which lifelong education might
be organized.  Clearly, people at different ages interact with
reality in differing ways, small children, for example, learning primarily through concrete experience, abstract and formal-
ly-logical thinking developing later.  Consequently, it is apparent that classroom materials, student activities, evaluative
procedures, and so on, should all reflect the phenomena of cognitive growth.  This fact is fairly well recognized in existing
systems.

However, analysis of the nature of cognitive growth also
indicates that, quite apart from age-related phenomena, different people show different patterns of cognitive functioning.
Some prefer information to be transmitted in broad generalizations.  Others operate best when it is embedded in a supporting
context.  Some people grasp fine details readily, but may not
notice the underlying general structure, some have difficulty
with details, but can grasp the broad outline with ease.  Some
people prefer information to be presented in abstract forms,
some learn best in a concrete situation.  Some prefer words,
some deeds, and so on.  Consequently, it is important that more
attention be paid to the cognitive properties of learners than
is currently the case.  In particular, a system is called for
in which many modalities are used for transmitting information.
This would include learning through listening, through doing,
through watching, through living, through working, through
teaching others, and so on.

## Chapter 6

# Integration of Social, Motivational and Affective Development

## CONCEPTS IN SOCIO-AFFECTIVE DEVELOPMENT

*The socio-affective domain*

The term "socio-affective" is used here to refer to those aspects of psychological function which involve interactions with other people on the one hand, and moods, feelings, self-image, goals, aspirations and motivations on the other. Socio-affective functioning is thus distinguished from intellectual functioning with its emphasis on skills and abilities, and from cognitive functioning with its emphasis on techniques and styles of interacting with information. Just as intellectual and cognitive development have been described as characterized by an interacting sequence of changes, it will be shown in the present chapter that socio-affective development involves a similar pattern of change. Socio-affective development is to be seen in changes in social roles during life, changes in aspirations and expectations, changes in what are perceived as goals and rewards, changes in how the self is seen to be related to other people, to work or to life itself, and in other similar changes. The underlying premise of the chapter is that social skills, patterns of motivation, affective resources, personality, and sense of self, among others, are both vertically and horizontally integrated. In other words, development in these domains both rests upon earlier development and also serves as the base for later development, while social, motivational and affective domains modify and in turn are modified by each other.

*Horizontal integration of socio-affective functioning*

Social, motivational and affective functioning cannot be thought of as three distinct sets of discrete functions that

95

operate in isolation from each other.  Quite the opposite is
the case.  For example, learning is modified by motivation; it
has become almost a truism that motivated learning is superior
to unmotivated learning (see Biggs, 1968, for a typical discussion).  It has also been demonstrated that both learning and
motivation are affected by emotion, so that, for example, in a
state of heightened emotion, increased motivation may render
behaviour rigid and disorganized, with the result that learning
is impaired.  This inter-relationship of learning, affect and
motivation has been summarized in the "Yerkes-Dodson-Law".  In
its simplest form, this law states that, at high levels of task
difficulty, learning is inhibited by increased motivation,
whereas at low levels of task difficulty, it may be improved
by increased motivation.  The interaction among learning, motivation and affect is non-linear, and follows the inverted U-
curve shown in the figure below.

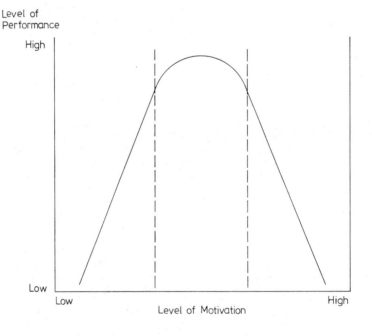

Fig. 5.   Relationship between motivation
          and level of performance

Figure 5 also shows that it is possible to discern zones
of less-than-optimal motivation (i.e., the area to the left of
the broken vertical dividing line), and areas of above-optimal
motivation (i.e., the area to the right of the center line).
In situations where the present level of motivation and/or affect is below-optimal, increased motivation improves learning
By contrast, where the present level of motivation and/or affect is higher-than-optimal, increased motivation inhibits
learning. However, interaction is more complex than this. Affective levels may modify judgmental and perceptual processes,
with a resulting change in the perception of motivating factors.
It is appropriate to conceptualize an individual person as a
highly-organized reciprocal network of psychological functions
that operate on each other, in an extremely complex way.

*Vertical integration*

Socio-affective functioning is also integrated over time.
With increasing psychological development, people acquire patterns of motives, the capacity to experience emotions, an image
of themselves as a certain kind of a person, and so on.  Each
phase of development in these domains is linked to preceding
phases and to subsequent phases, so that events at one time in
the developmental process interact with those at both earlier
and later times.  This sequence of changes has often been conceptualized as a series of stages of life.  The concept of life
as a sequence of changes is by no means new.  Examination of
philosophical writings and poetry dating back to antiquity contains references to the idea (Asian Institute, 1970).  However,
in more recent years, a number of formal descriptive systems
have been developed to provide a systematic framework within
which to examine social, affective and motivational development.
The analysis that follows is organized in terms of a number of
these frameworks.

*The curve of life*

According to Bühler (1935), it is possible to discern
"...a regular sequence in the events, experiences and attain-
ments in life...".  She saw this sequence as arranged in a systematic manner such that three phases could be discerned, a
phase of expansion during childhood and early adulthood, a
phase of stability in the prime of life years, and a phase of
restriction in old age.  This led her to talk of a "curve of
life" which could be used to summarize graphically the shape of

socio-affective development. This curve, with its three phases, resembles the smoothed, generalized curve of intellectual growth presented in Chapter 4 (see p. 55). However, in her more recent writings, Bühler has revised her earlier conceptualization of adulthood. Initially, she described it as a plateau period (stability) which led into the collapse of old age (restriction), but more recently she has acknowledged that adulthood is a legitimate stage of life itself, rather than a period of holding on prior to decline. She now describes socio-affective development as having two complete repetitions of the cycle of self-realization, one as an adult, one as a child (Bühler, 1962). Thus, she has recognized that socio-affective development extends far beyond childhood, and that adulthood is a legitimate phase in the process itself, rather than merely a prolonged afternoon following childhood's bright dawn, before the onset of the twilight of old age.


*Erikson's stage theory*

    According to Erikson (e.g. 1959), there are eight stages of life, ranging from infancy through early childhood, to young adulthood, adulthood and old age. His work has subsequently been interpreted and somewhat revised by Peck (1956) who has enunciated some of the key traits of middle age and old age. These traits are of considerable interest to the present document. Middle age is characterized by a switch in values from emphasis on physical power to emphasis on wisdom. Similarly, social values switch from "sexualizing" to socializing, while emotional life is characterized by greatly increased flexibility. With old age, the transition from the concern with mastery and achievement which is at its peak in young adults is completed. Under ideal conditions, the self is valued above work and achievement, there is transcendence over one's body, and ultimately, transcendence over one's self. Thus, as in Bühler's later writings, it is clear that the characteristics of later years are treated much more positively in this conceptualization. Shifts in values and emphases with increasing age are described not as the failure of youth, but as the mastery of new levels of transcendence. Interestingly, this formulation is clearly consistent with studies of intellectual abilities indicating that the young are quick and sure in motor tasks, but that with age comes increasing mastery of reflective skills involving vocabulary, verbal reasoning, and so on (see Chapter 4).

*Havighurst and "developmental tasks"*

According to Havighurst (e.g. 1953), socio-affective development is mainly a matter of mastery of "tasks" such as learning to relate to other people, or mastering a sex role. The tasks are hierarchically ordered, with self-preservation tasks at the lowest level, self-fulfilment tasks at the highest. When the struggle to survive is predominant, little mastery of higher-order self-realization tasks occurs. The tasks are systematically ordered by age, too, with certain kinds of task being predominant at one stage of development, but not at another. For example, learning a sex role is not a major task for newborns or for the very old, but it is a major problem which adolescents must overcome (i.e. it is an important developmental task during adolescence). Havighurst discerned six broad stages of socio-affective development, each stage being unified by the primacy of similar "dominant concerns". He specified approximate age ranges for the various stages. These are reproduced in Table 1 and provide a useful terminological framework for discussing socio-affective development.

TABLE 1

Havighurst's Six Developmental Stages

| Stage | Approx. Age Limits |
|---|---|
| 1. Infancy and Early Childhood | 0 - 6  years |
| 2. Middle Childhood | 6 - 12 years |
| 3. Adolescence | 12 - 18 years |
| 4. Early Adulthood | 18 - 30 years |
| 5. Middle Age | 30 - 35 years |
| 6. Later Maturity | 55 +    years |

*Adulthood as a stage of life*

Many other concepts for systematizing the study of socio-affective development exist. However, the intention of the present section is not to review them all, nor to provide an exhaustive survey of theories of psychological development. The major object is to indicate that there is strong recognition of the fact that socio-affective development is, indeed,

a developmental process, along with an increasing awareness of
the autonomous status of adulthood as a phase in the developmental process, rather than as a half-way house between childhood (where most emphasis in developmental psychology has been
placed) and senility (where some growing interest is now becoming apparent). The increasing interest in adulthood, and
the existence of a felt need for clearer conceptual systems for
organizing study of adulthood, can be seen in the recent attempt of Houle and Houle (1970) to sub-divide the adult period
into a number of sub-stages, each needing special study of its
own, and each characterized by a distinctive developmental status. They suggested that adulthood consists of six stages,
which they called respectively "onset of maturity", "young
adulthood", "early middle age", "later middle age", "old age",
and "senescence".

## DEVELOPMENT DURING THE DIFFERENT STAGES OF LIFE

Examination of the various theoretical formulations concerning socio-affective development indicates that there is
wide-spread agreement on a number of its characteristics, despite disagreements in specific details from writer to writer.
The following pages contain a summary of the main features of
socio-affective development, unifying into a single broad framework the various descriptions that exist in the literature.
This description is organized around three broad areas: social
roles; aspirations, goals and rewards; motivation.

*Social roles*

During childhood young children are dependent and relatively powerless, in terms of the society as a large group.
Their role is that of recipient of what those who control resources (food, clean diapers, etc.) supply. They are expected
to be led by adults and to train themselves for the future.
They are treated as essentially helpless and in need of protection, and as basically incapable of making important decisions for themselves. This role may be so strongly imposed by
some parents that they seem to oppose, on principle, any positive decision-making role on the part of their children, apparently following the dictum that children are so incompetent
that any decision they make is bound to be wrong. Children do
not always endorse the role that society assigns to them. Indeed, refusal to accept the passive, dependent role, especially
on the part of adolescents, is a prime factor in inter-genera-

tional conflict that is common (or at least widely publicized) nowadays. Nonetheless, the conventional role for children is that of dependency and powerlessness.

In adolescence the beginnings of the adult role of wage-earner and pillar of the community begin to be laid down. At this stage of socio-affective development, a problem arises in some societies in which the status of the adolescent segment of the population may be obscure because, although its members are physically and biologically adult, they are still confined to the role of children by the society. This problem is particularly acute in highly-developed societies which require a lengthy period of childhood (usually a period of education) for the acquisition of the advanced skills needed for eventual graduation into the role of adult and bread-winner. By contrast, in some other societies, the transition is clearcut, with childhood terminating abruptly on the occasion of formal admission to adult status through some kind of initiation ceremony or puberty rite.

During early adulthood, the role of parent and rising leader of the society is paramount. Just what ages encompass "early adulthood" may vary widely, just as the ages of childhood vary from society to society. Although the rationale being developed here is mainly based on urban, technologically-advanced, white societies of Western-European origin, flexibility on the part of the reader in making the necessary adjustments and allowances will permit emergence of a relatively typical, general description of development which describes the process in many widely differing societies. Young adults are expected to participate vigorously in the strenuous and gainful activities of the society, and establish themselves as stable members capable of functioning within its particular requirements and constraints. In middle adulthood, more concern for community works, guidance of the young, social service, and so on, is appropriate. In Western European societies the role of leader of the family, respecter of the traditional verities, and friend of the community is appropriate for middle-class males, and a similar role *mutatis mutandis* for females. In this stage of life, people are expected to display leadership in politics, committee membership, acceptance of positions of trust in Church and Unions and so on. As late adulthood and then old age supervene, the individual is expected to become increasingly passive and dependent, to become markedly less vigorous and thrusting in relationships with society, and to yield to the new, upcoming social elements. To some extent, the wheel swings full circle, in that the roles assigned to the elderly are, in many ways, comparable with those assigned to the very young.

*Aspirations, goals and rewards*

A very similar cyclical pattern can be seen in other socio-affective areas. Childhood is marked by development of a stable identity, differentiation of self from environment, and so on. Needs and goals are short-term and concrete (food, entertainment, etc.), and there is minimal ability to delay gratifications. With adolescence comes greater preoccupation with social identity - with finding a job, developing a stable and coherent "ideology", establishing a sex role and so on. Many goals are long-term, and there is a pronounced orientation towards the future. There is much interest in self-image, and metaphysical issues assume considerable importance (e.g. issues like "Who am I?", "Why am I here?", "Where am I going?" and so on). This aspect of adolescent functioning is demonstrated by the peaking of interest in religion during that period, great concern with human rights and justice, and so on.

In early adulthood, there is great interest in child-rearing, and a vigorous attack on carving out one's place in the world, for example through consolidation of job skills. Interest tends to switch to immediate, relatively concrete issues, rather than the abstract problems with which the adolescent was concerned. Energy is focused on consolidating one's position and getting ahead. By middle adulthood these kinds of issue tend to have been settled. Child rearing may be past, some kind of job stability has been achieved and issues such as serving society, and preserving what is treasured, begin to dominate. For women, an important factor is that children no longer need continual care, so that they may return to the job market or seek interesting activities. Both men and women show interest in developing new careers at this stage, as a result of the reduction in concern over "proving themselves", protecting a family, and so on. Late adulthood and old age involve increasing concern with short-term goals, a growing sense that the world is a difficult, complex organization full of problems, and resurgence of metaphysical interests. With old age comes increasing social isolation, disengagement from active struggle, concentration on passive, contemplative pursuits, and great concern for short-term, concrete goals such as food and ways to pass the time pleasantly.

*Motivation*

As with other areas of socio-affective development, the domain of motivation shows a sequential set of changes with passage through the adult years. Motivation may be defined, in a nutshell, as willingness to focus effort. Where people are willing to expend a great deal of energy on seeking a particular goal, they are said to be motivated to achieve that goal. Kuhlen (1963) has suggested that there are two broad meta-motives in adult development. One of these broad motives is a drive towards expansion and growth. This motive is seen in the seeking of achievement and power in the inter-personal domain, and in self-fulfilment and self-perpetuation (for example through sexual reproduction or other means of rendering oneself immortal) in the intra-personal domain. This pattern of motivation is strongest in early adulthood and begins to wane after about age 50, although it is still clearly visible in some people until age 60 or beyond.

The other broad motive Kuhlen discerned is the opposite of that just described. It involves the selection of goals as a result of the motivating thrust of anxiety and insecurity. This broad kind of motivation has several forms including motivation to deal with self-perceived psychological inadequacies, unhappiness, social inadequacy, lack of identity, and physical distress. It is relatively less prominent (although obviously still present) among young adults than the first kind of motivation, but accounts for a larger proportion of motivation with increasing age, gaining in importance as the expansion and growth pattern decreases.

It is clear that both kinds of motivation are present over the entire adult age span, so that it is not a matter of one replacing the other, but rather of their relative importance changing with age, roughly approximating the loss of physical power, desirability as an employee, sensory acuity, socially-determined personal beauty, and so on, which accompany increasing age. Broadly speaking, young adults are primarily motivated by desire for mastery and personal achievement, older adults by desire to avoid inadequacy in many domains. It is important to ask, however, to what extent this developmental pattern in the motivational domain is socially determined (for example by a social definition of the middle-aged as unemployable, and the consequent need for people of 50 or so to stave off unemployment). This issue will be taken up again in a later section.

*Interaction in socio-affective development*

The developmental progression has several major characteristics which must be re-stressed for the present purposes. It is sequential, in that subsequent steps arise out of and partly depend on earlier ones. For example, re-opening of interest in

metaphysical issues and pursuit of social-service goals would
be greatly facilitated by establishment of a clear psychological identity, perception of oneself as capable and successful,
and even such concrete factors as achieving some degree of fi-
nancial-vocational success and getting the children through
adolescence and into early adulthood. The ability to affect
other people's behaviour and play a leader's role would be facilitated by successful mastery of the culture's key social
skills, and so on. The sequence is also interactive with the
environment, in that, not only does development at any stage
depend on feedback, but the nature and extent of earlier adjustments will affect the kind of feedback that is received. For
example, a person who behaves in ways which a society regards
as neurotic or criminal will, in trying to offer leadership,
receive different patterns of response from other people than
would have been the case had previous behaviour been unobjec-
tionable.

It is also striking that the nature of environmental demands tends to modify social roles, goals and aspirations, and
motivations. Thus, for example, some of the features of behaviour during early childhood and during old age are quite
similar. Although the tendency of the elderly to concentrate
on short-term goals is no doubt affected by their knowledge
that they do not have 20 or 30 years ahead of them for which to
plan, the broad similarity in the demands that society makes on
the very old and the very young (i.e. the similar roles that it
assigns to the two groups), in that both are expected to be
dependent, passive, socially-isolated, and so on, may well interact with the physical weakness which characterizes both age
groups to yield stereotyped behaviours from them (e.g. Comfort,
1967).

## FACTORS INFLUENCING SOCIO-AFFECTIVE DEVELOPMENT

*Nature versus nurture*

Observation of the everyday world leaves a strong impres-
sion that children grow up to resemble their parents. In fact,
the idea that the course of development in children is at least
partly determined by their parentage is so time-honoured that
it may appear to need little documentation. The early, formal
studies of the origins of psychological development emphasized
very strongly the effects of blood lines, or what is now called
heredity (nature). For example, although he made passing reference to the effects of environmental influences, Galton (1869)
concluded that the reasons why some people grew up to be judges,

bishops or generals lay primarily in their heredity. Similarly,
turn-of-the-century longitudinal studies of the development of
intelligence emphasized the importance of heredity. Dugdale
(1887) assumed that the reason for the consistent appearance of
socially maladjusted behaviour in a single family he studied
(the Jukes family) was a result of bad breeding. Similarly,
Goddard (1912) blamed heredity for the different patterns of
psychological development seen in two lines of descent from the
same father (Martin Kallikak) by two different women. The children of one of the women, a respectable young lady of Boston,
grew up to become highly respected citizens and successful professional men, while the children stemming from a liaison with
the other woman, a feeble-minded tavern maid, grew up to become
liars, thieves and criminals. In both cases, interpretations
emphasized heredity, and little attention seems to have been
paid to the effects of environmental factors (nurture).

The roles of heredity and environment, for example in the
development of intelligence, have been a matter of dispute for
many years. Studies of twins reared together and apart such
as those of Burt (e.g. 1966) have not been able to establish
conclusively the primacy of heredity or environment. Almost
invariably, twin studies have indicated that intelligence test
scores are influenced both by hereditary factors and by environment. For instance, identical twins reared together resemble each other more than do ordinary siblings (an effect usually attributed to the effects of heredity) but, when reared
apart, they resemble each other less than when reared together
(apparently because of environmental differences). Research
in this area in recent years has switched from questions like
"Which is more important in psychological growth, heredity or
environment?" to focus on the way heredity and environment
interact in guiding growth (e.g. Anastasi 1958). Briefly, it
is currently accepted that both heredity and environment are
important. Their joint action should not be conceptualized as
involving two independent sets of factors which add together
to form a total effect. Rather, heredity and environment interact with each other in shaping development. For example, the
absence of an appropriate hereditary predisposition can negate
environmental influences highly-facilitative of a certain pattern of growth. On the other hand, absence of appropriate environmental stimuli can prevent a strong hereditary predisposition
from taking effect. One cannot disentangle the two sets of
influences and assign differential degrees of importance to
them. In a sense both heredity and environment are each 100%
responsible for development.

*Effects of environmental factors*

Possibly the most powerful environmental influence is provided by the framework of social institutions within which people live their lives - what is usually called their "society"
or "culture". As McLeish (1963, p. 23) has pointed out, the
child is initially amoral and poorly coordinated to the requirements of the social environment. A major feature of subsequent
development involves learning to function within a society.
McLeish (p. 85) calls this "learning to conform". The role of
societal factors in cognitive development is particularly clear.
These effects have been most strongly emphasized by Bruner and
Vygotsky, whose theories of cognitive growth have been sketched
out briefly in earlier sections (see Chapter 5). The key point
for the present analysis is that the ways in which people learn
to process information received from the world in which they
live is partly determined by the conventions of the societies
in which they grow up. Vernon (1969), for example has summarized some of the evidence which shows that even perceptual
processes such as the susceptibility to certain kinds of visual
illusion seem to be culturally modified. Furthermore, as his
research within a variety of cultures has shown, certain kinds
of intellectual ability may be highly developed and commonplace
in some societies, but virtually absent in others. Ferguson
(1954) has strongly emphasized the role of society in intellectual development, suggesting that what we call "intelligence"
is really a set of skills learned as a result of coping with a
particular society and is, therefore, highly culture-bound. A
similar point of view has been put forward by Fischer (1969).
Again, Schubert and Cropley (1972) have argued that cultural
traditions for processing experience greatly influence the
kinds of intellectual task which people from different cultures
can carry out efficiently. Societal effects on psychological
growth are not however, confined to the cognitive domain. The
effect of social influences on attitudes and values has also
been emphasized by various writers. Comfort (1970) argued that
cultural expectations shape people's attitudes. For example,
rigidity and flexibility in middle age may reflect society's
belief about what people are like at that age, rather than any
inherent tendency. Gintis (1971) has referred to the role of
family factors in shaping socio-affective functioning, attitudes to school, learning and society, as have a whole series
of recent studies of differential school achievement (e.g.
Bloom, 1976; Coleman, 1966; Jenks, 1972).

*The economic environment and psychological growth*

One feature of society which is important in guiding psychological growth is its economic organization. Stated very simply, "the economy" may be thought of as the system for producing and distributing goods and services. Participation in this system provides employment, income and purchasing power. It also provides opportunities to define oneself in terms of work-related roles, to find a level of functioning (e.g. as a boss, a humble functionary, etc.), and so on. The economic organization of society thus provides a system of financial and non-financial rewards for the people who participate in it. A history of uninterrupted employment, steady promotion, successful completion of job-related tasks, and so on, is likely to foster a sense of personal worth, competence and confidence. On the other hand, a history of unemployment, job failure and low wages is likely to foster a different pattern of attitudes and motivations. Work is capable of providing a sense of achievement, a feeling of being creative, a feeling of being of service, a place to make friends, a place to enjoy human companionship, and so on (Friedmann and Havighurst, 1954), or it may have an opposite function.

It is apparent, then, that the kinds of personality development described in earlier sections are intimately related to the economic organization of a society. Job success reinforces and strengthens feelings of competence and worthwhileness such as are seen in the adult stage of personality development. Economic failure, on the other hand, makes development of such feelings very difficult. To take another example, social expectations of retirement at age 65 provide a powerful environmental influence fostering feelings of helplessness and waning power in adults reaching the period of "restriction" in personality development. If compulsory retirement is accompanied by the notion that the person approaching retirement is worn-out and useless, personality deterioration would be accelerated, and the shutting-off of intellectual activities strongly encouraged. In a similar vein, where work involved no active participation on the part of the worker, apart from carrying out the necessary physical movements involved in the job, it would also be poorly attuned to the growth of a sense of personal satisfaction, confidence in the future, etc.

*Lifelong education and the work environment*

Work is a major economic aspect of life which interacts in an important way with schooling. When a society stresses that

children go to school in order to be supplied with the knowledge needed for the life ahead, the school-work system will
tend to operate as a closed, self-perpetuating circle, as a result of which schooling serves merely to "reproduce the relations of production" (Bowles, 1971, p. 178).   In such a context,
work would tend to inhibit lifelong learning.   However, one of
the main principles of lifelong education is the forging of a
link between learning and work, so that the place of work becomes a place of learning, not a place in which learning ceases.
Workers habitually produce knowledge during their daily work;
they produce solutions, improve their skills, try out new modes
of production, and so on.   However, this is seldom recognized,
because the education provided by work, and the contribution
of workers as teachers both of themselves and of each other, is
taken for granted and rarely subjected to serious study.
        At present, learning through work is seldom sufficiently
analyzed or subjected to improvement through research and coordination, apparently because, since it is not provided by
people formally identified as teachers (it is "only" provided
by fellow workers), it is regarded as trivial (UNESCO, 1976).
By contrast, in a system organized according to the principles
of lifelong education, the close relationship between work, the
socio-economic organization of society, and education would be
strongly emphasized, and many hitherto neglected places and
modes of learning given due emphasis.


*The social environment*

        Within a given person, ideas, feelings, attitudes, values,
motives and self-image become stable as the person develops.
Each individual's behaviour becomes relatively consistent and
coherent.   Although a given person's behaviour is not fixed or
predetermined as a result of this tendedy to behave consistently, it is apparent that there are limits within which each
individual normally functions.   On the other hand, the pattern
of psychological organization characteristic of a given person
has many idiosyncratic features which make it unique and dis-
tinguishable from that of other people, so that each person
possesses a distinct internally consistent *modus operanti*. This
band or spectrum of behaviours within which an individual functions is said to result from possession of a particular "personality" (e.g. McDavid and Harari, 1968).   Although it is common
to acknowledge the role of hereditary factors in the development of personality (e.g. Gottesman, 1963), the characteristic
ways in which people express their own individuality in dealing

with the environment (their personality) is very largely argued to be a result of the process of socialization (e.g.,
Sontag, Baker and Nelson, 1958). Thus, the social environment
in which a person grows up conditions psychological growth.
Within a given society, there is a good deal of consensus
concerning what are the correct ways of doing things, what are
good and bad habits, appropriate attitudes and motives, and so
on. Consequently, most of the members of a particular society
are subjected to much the same socialization processes, and the
result is the emergence of a relatively standard set of values,
attitudes, beliefs and behaviours within each society. Deviations between individuals are common, but these deviations lie
within certain limits that are tolerated by the society. The
society also determines within which areas of life deviation
from the norm will be most readily permitted, within which areas conformity will be most demanded, and so on. Thus, society
has a stereotype of what people should be like which, while it
may describe no single individual person in great detail, em-
bodies an outline of the kind of person the society regards as
"right".
    As a result, by growing up in a particular society, in-
dividuals acquire a set of common goals, aspirations, beliefs,
values, and so on. They learn what kind of people they are and
what their duties and privileges are. What it means to be a member of a given society may be stressed in that society's life
in poem, song and folklore, in the legends and stories which
children are told, or even in formal statutes. Endorsement
and acceptance of the national self-image involves substantial
rewards. People understand clearly what they ought to do to be
worthwhile persons, what they can expect from other people,
what it is proper and fitting for them to aspire to, how their
lives may be expected to develop, and so on. As Circautas
(1957) has pointed out, the reward for conformity to the expectations of society is that one can function "without undue
strain". The penalties of faulty socialization are demonstrated
by the trials of the immigrant who finds that even the simplest
actions like, say, riding on a bus, may be fraught with difficulty and uncertainty.
    It is not uncommon to find this process of adoption and
endorsement of a society's values described in uncomplimentary
terms as "mere conformity" (e.g. McLeish, 1963). However, as
Kovacs and Cropley (1975) have shown, impaired ability to function easily and smoothly within a given social context can lead
to psychological discomfort, unhappiness, and even severe psy-
chopathological states. The advantage of socialization is ease
of function in a particular society. The disadvantage is the

necessity to endorse at least partly a pre-determined set of
judgments as to one's role in life, what one may reasonably
aspire to, what are good and what bad behaviours, how one
should behave towards various other groups of people, and so
on.  The agencies through which societies achieve socialization
of their members are of considerable importance in attitudes to
school, education and lifelong learning.


*Lifelong education and the cultural environment*

      The new demands and pressures exerted on people's values,
motives and self-image go beyond the vocational domain,  A wave
of political, social and scientific change is also sweeping
across all nations, perhaps even more deeply in developing than
in developed countries.  Values, interpersonal relations, life
roles, the very idea of what is meant by a purposeful and productive existence are now uncertain.  Such widespread changes
in the socio-cultural environment pose the threat of increasing
uncertainty, overwhelming of individuality, and deepening alienation.
      The positive reaction to this state of affairs involves in-
creasing demand for a dynamic, as against a static, culture, in
which people have a say in decisions affecting not only work,
but also home and social life, leisure activities, self-expression, and so on.  Current educational systems often fail to reflect, in their curricula, the richness of contemporary cultural expression, and especially that of peasants or workers.  However, lifelong education's emphasis on links with work, leisure,
community action -- the kinds of activities through which people in the street form their opinions and express their thoughts
and feelings -- would make it possible for schools to be directly involved with the needs, aspirations, hopes, wishes and modes
of self-expression of the society in which they live, in the
form that these aspects of popular culture are developed and
experienced by the members of the society.  Thus, they have the
potential to foster a constructive educational reaction to the
problems and dangers of the times, helping individuals to develop insight into the cultural problems of their society, and
feelings of control over their future as producers, consumers,
citizens and creators (UNESCO, 1976).
      The link between lifelong education and the popular culture
also takes a second form.  It is easy to take the pronouncements
of academics, educational reformers, and politicians too seriously when drastic innovations in education are being considered.
However, it should be borne in mind that the ultimate determi-

nant of what reforms can be made and which aspects of the innovations will persist is not the theory of the scholars, the
classroom practices of the reformers, or the declaiming of the
politicians, but the willingness of the public at large to accept some changes, whereas others are rejected (Duke, 1976).
Thus, lifelong education will only become a reality when it is
accepted by the people in the street; i.e., when it is absorbed
into and becomes an integral part of their culture (UNESCO,
1976).


*The family*

    The young child's first contact with the socializing agen-
cies of society is normally provided by interactions with parents.  In the usual state of affairs, the parents will themselves have experienced a process of socialization of perhaps
30 or more years' duration.  As a result, they will normally
endorse a particular set of values and attitudes characteristic
of the society in which they live.  Even among parents who regard themselves as "liberal" or "modern", there will be a high
level of endorsement of certain basic social premises, very frequently without any realization of that fact.  From the beginning, then, children will be trained in the ways of society,
and will be rewarded for accepting its definition of what they
should be like.  For example, in some societies, they will almost immediately begin to be fed an artificial diet, possibly
on the grounds that breast feeding is of low social status, bad
for the mother's bodily beauty, or for some other reason.  They
may be trained to be quiet and passive, possibly by being tight-
ly bound almost continuously, or to be energetic and vigorous,
by being left unswaddled and unconfined.  Their toilet training
will begin almost immediately according to the tradition of
their society.  Extremely "hygienic" practices are prevalent in
some (e.g. the use of diapers, constant cleaning and so on),
while in others little notice is taken of the baby's elimina-
tory functions.
    As the child develops, subtle training in many of the val-
ues of the society will occur.  For example, without necessarily having the slightest consciousness of doing so, the parents
may teach the child a highly defined set of social roles.  The
very selection of toys which are offered to the young child may
reflect differential reinforcement for the adoption of certain
roles, so that boys may be given tools and weapons, girls tiny
household implements. As Bandura and others have shown (Bandura
and Walters, 1963), children acquire many behaviours simply

by observing their parents. In this way, a little girl may quickly learn that she is restricted to certain levels of aspiration, certain defined areas of personal development, and so on, while a little boy may be taught quite different roles.

Within a given society, the socialization processes may be further organized according to sub-systems within it such as socio-economic class. Thus, in a Western-European society, middle-class children may be rewarded for verbal precocity and a disposition to spend their spare time reading books, while working-class children may be rewarded for physical prowess, vigorous self-assertion and so on. Although the dichotomy just described is by no means perfectly correlated with socio-economic status, there is a tendency for the children of white-collar workers to receive the first pattern of reinforcement, those of manual workers, the second pattern. Thus, through one of its most powerful agencies, the family, society guides and modifies psychological development in children in a wide variety of areas of interest to the present chapter. For example, they are taught to confine their aspirations to certain occupational levels, to expect themselves to acquire only certain levels of certain kinds of skill, to prepare themselves for specified social roles, to attend school for only specified periods, and so on. They are also taught that certain kinds of cognitive function are desirable, certain undesirable, and that school is or is not an agency which is capable of furthering their aspirations. In fact, people are taught in a general way what is expected of them and what they are capable of. So important is this training that major studies (Jencks, 1972; Plowden, 1967) have concluded that it is one of the main determinants of the child's reaction to subsequent schooling.

*Lifelong education and the family*

One of the most powerful phenomena seen in contemporary educational reform is the gradual change over from elitist forms of schooling to a kind that is more universally available, a change which has reached different levels in different countries. Many children are now receiving schooling at levels higher than those reached by their parents. One result of this has been an increase in parents' interest in their children's schooling, especially in countries where the increased education has resulted in a direct financial burden for the parents, as for example in many developing countries. This has, in turn, been associated in many countries with the growth of parents' associations, village educational councils, and similar bodies

(UNESCO, 1976).  However, parental involvement has often encountered opposition from teachers and administrators, with resulting resistance from parents, and attempts on their part to
impose teaching methods, evaluation procedures and the like.
Thus, family and school have sometimes been at loggerheads.

By contrast, lifelong education emphasizes co-operation
between family and school in the sharing of a joint educational
experience.  Proponents of lifelong education accept the cultural individuality of the family, and stress its importance as
one of the most important educative agencies in the society.
Within the family itself there is an important and significant
educational process -- it is the main learning environment for
very young children, transmits many crucial basic skills, builds
attitudes to work and leisure, and many more.  The theory of
lifelong education recognizes that an enlightened family life
has the potential to lay down a basic framework of emancipation
of spirit, enthusiasm and skill which will transform the whole
life of the individual.  For this reason, it is very important
that school curriculum consciously seek to build links with the
family (Skager and Dave, 1977).

## SCHOOLING AND SOCIO-AFFECTIVE DEVELOPMENT

*School as a socializing agency*

Although psychological development obviously occurs with
or without formal education, it is clear that many societies
regard school as one of the major socializing agencies.  Indeed,
paedagogical textbooks frequently contain professions of faith
in the school as an instrument of social change.  Teachers are
expected to display "desirable" behaviours and to act as an
idealized model of what the society (or at least those elements
of it which are responsible for the hiring and firing of teachers) deem to be "correct" behaviour.  Preambles to curricula
frequently state as secondary or even primary goals the incul-
cation of desirable value systems, aspirations and attitudes.
Very large portions of the national budget are frequently ex-
pended on education, and educational systems are constructed
and regulated according to very elaborate and systematic bodies
of law.  Thus, perhaps next to the family, the single social
agency in which the highest hopes are placed, and certainly the
one on which the greatest expenditures of time and money are
made, is that of formal schooling.  Whether these hopes and expectations are justified, however, is another matter.

*Loss of confidence in the school*

Attempts to show that there are differences in pupil outcomes of formal education which are closely correlated with
either teacher differences (e.g. Jansen, Jansen and Mylov, 1972;
Soar, 1972) or differences in school facilities (e.g. Jencks,
1972) have had disappointing and surprising results.  In general, these kinds of study have tended to show that factors
like family background and personality are as important as
school-related factors in determining school outcomes.  Such
conclusions are not confined to studies in the United States,
but apparently also apply to less technologically-advanced countries (Simmons and Erkut, 1972).  In a similar vein, studies
like those of Berg (1970), Selowsky (1968) and Jencks (1972)
have all suggested that the real-life benefits accruing to students of differing educational backgrounds are only weakly related to school factors.  They are much more strongly related
to difference in attitudes and motivations such as are inculcated by family background.  Gintis (1971) has, in fact, suggested that the major benefit of schooling, as far as real-life
outcomes are concerned, lies in non-cognitive training received
there, for example, in determination and endurance.

*Schooling and socio-affective functioning*

There are, then, grounds for believing that real-life differences among students of differing educational backgrounds
are not primarily the result of cognitive training received in
school, but, rather, result from the school's ability to
strengthen pre-existing or concurrently developed attitudes
and values.  School may also help students to crystallize attitudes which have been only weakly inculcated by other components of the society.  Finally, school may legitimize certain
values and attitudes, by appearing to give them authoritative
endorsement.  Thus, it may be said to increase pre-existing
differences among students rather than to reduce them.  Cognitively, school apparently functions primarily by offering a
site for the acquisition of cognitive skills, and a socio-affective context in which that acquisition occurs.  The actual
rate of development of cognitive skills by different pupils,
however, is very largely determined by their previous patterns
of socialization.  Findings like those of Jencks do not indicate that children learn nothing at school, but that how much
they learn, what they learn and at what rate they learn, are
determined by out-of-school experiences as much as by in-school
experience.

Nevertheless, school is itself an important socializing agency which is capable of modifying psychological functioning. In a series of early studies, Anderson and his colleagues (Anderson, 1939; Anderson and Brewer, 1945, 1946; Anderson, Brewer and Reed, 1946) showed, for example, that classroom organization can foster initiative, responsibility and independent problem-solving if it is of an appropriate kind. Similarly, Soar (1972) showed that appropriate teacher behaviour can discourage or encourage dependent behaviour in pupils. He also showed that certain patterns of teacher criticism are related to the development of anxiety and dependence in students. On the other hand, Brophy and Good (1970) found that teachers can foster openness to new experiences and a continuing high level of motivation for further learning. Thus, it is apparent that differential patterns of teacher behaviour do have some effects in fostering different patterns of attitudes,values and motives in students.

*Socio-affective development and lifelong education*

This fact is of considerable importance in defining a psychological role for school in a lifelong education-oriented educational system. Continued learning is hampered by acceptance of stereotypes which suggest that formal learning is confined to the school years. Such stereotypes are reinforced by lack of motivation for continued learning, negative attitudes to oneself as a learner, and so on. Despite recent loss of confidence in schooling as an instrument for equalizing the cognitive benefits resulting from education, schools are apparently capable of exerting an influence in the areas of motivation and attitudes. Thus, to the extent that socio-affective functioning is a major factor in lifelong education, appropriate re-organization of formal education to encourage a favourable socio-affective basis for lifelong education may be of great importance in fostering lifelong learning.

This means that adoption of lifelong education as a formal principle for the organization of schooling would require an emphasis on the qualitative, rather than the quantitative aspects of schooling. That is to say, lifelong education-oriented schooling would place much emphasis on the role of school in fostering styles and patterns of function of an appropriate kind. A lifelong education-oriented curriculum would be much concerned with developing in pupils willingness to learn, acceptance of learning as a natural and desirable activity, positive definition of oneself as a learner, and so on.

# Chapter 7

# Implications of Lifelong
# Education for Curriculum

## THE LIFELONG LEARNER

Prior to discussion of the major design features of a life-long education-oriented curriculum, it is appropriate to ask what a lifelong learner would be like. For the purposes of the present text, the answer will be couched in psychological terms. The framework which will be employed is the tri-partite model which has been touched upon earlier. The lifelong learner may be considered psychologically in intellectual, cognitive, and motivational/socio-affective terms. In the intellectual and cognitive domains, a fusion of the material analyzing the concept of lifelong education and that outlining the course of psychological growth indicates that lifelong learners would treat knowledge as a continuous fabric of a cumulative nature, with present knowledge serving as the basis for future cognitive growth. They would relate new information to a broad general framework, and continually integrate new knowledge into that framework. They would be well equipped with knowledge-getting techniques, and would be thoroughly aware of the many sources of knowledge lying outside the classroom. More important, however, they would be skilled at *using* knowledge. They would be expected to understand that knowledge and information are an expanding network in which the parts continually interlock. This means, among other things, that although they might develop special expertise in a relatively limited area, specialization would be secondary to a broad grasp of the basic concepts.

As was shown in Chapter 4, a major factor limiting learning outside formal school settings lies in the motivational domain. Unfortunately, the ability to see change and uncertainty as challenges triggering adaptive, knowledge-getting behaviour is not necessarily well developed in all people. Motivationally speaking, the lifelong learner is the person who has

developed the capacity to be positively motivated by the need
for more learning. This positive motivation would be seen not
only across age levels within a given individual (i.e., vertically integrated), but it would also manifest itself in positive motivation to learning in a wide variety of settings in
life (i.e., it would be horizontally integrated too). The lifelong learner would continually seek change, novelty and personal growth. In the socio-affective domain, lifelong learners
would be expected to see themselves as learners both throughout
life (vertically), and also across the various domains of life
(i.e., horizontally). Continued learning would be enhancing
to the self-image, and would produce positive emotional experiences. In relationships with their fellows, they would be attracted by opportunities to play new social roles, willing to
abandon well-established social status, to develop membership
of new groups, and so on.

One summary of the psychological nature of the lifelong
learner is to be found in Table 2 (p. 118) which was developed
from Dave (1973, pp. 32-35). This table concentrates on cognitive and motivational properties.


## CAN SCHOOL DEVELOP LIFELONG LEARNERS?

It is clear from earlier chapters that the cognitive, motivational, and socio-affective make-up of individuals is a dynamic and developing property, which undergoes a process of growth
during life. A crucial question for the present analysis is
that of whether this developmental process is amenable to change
as a result of deliberate managing and structuring of experiences during the developmental sequence. Any discussion of
what a curriculum ought to be like to produce certain kinds of
people (in this case lifelong learners) is clearly based on the
belief that there is a relationship between the course of psychological development and the kinds of schooling that people
receive. If no such relationship existed, any talk about the
relative merits of a different curricular organization would be
entirely superfluous. For this reason, it is appropriate to
ask whether psychological development is affected by different
kinds of experiences, or whether the course of development is
predetermined and inevitable. If development followed a built-
in blueprint, there would be little point in designing different educational systems.

TABLE 2

Psychological Nature of the Lifelong Learner

---

Lifelong learners would be...

I  Cognitively well-equipped

-- familiar with a variety of disciplines and skills

-- familiar with the structures of knowledge, and not merely with facts

-- skilled at adapting the tools of learning and the structures of disciplines to new tasks

-- aware of the relationship between cognitive skills and real life

II  Highly educable

-- possessed of different learning strategies

-- able to learn in a variety of settings such as alone, in groups, and so on

-- well-equipped with basic learning skills such as reading, observing and listening, and able to understand non-verbal communication

-- well-equipped with basic intellectual skills such as reasoning, critical thinking and interpreting data

-- skilled at using many learning devices such as printed matter, mass media, and programmed materials

-- skilled at identifying their own learning needs

III Motivated to carry on a process of lifelong learning

-- aware of the rapidity of change and of its effects on social life, knowledge and job skills

-- aware that formal schooling is only the beginning of learning in life

-- aware of their personal responsibility to acquire new knowledge, skills and attitudes

-- aware of learning as a primary tool for personal and societal growth

---

*Environment and psychological development*

As Hunt (1973) has shown, early opinions in what might be called "modern" psychological thinking favoured the notion that the course of development is relatively fixed. Although writers such as Galton (1869) grudgingly acknowledged the effects of experience on psychological growth, there was, nonetheless, an overwhelming belief that the limits within which a person had the potential to vary as a result of experience were very narrow. In other words, it was believed that the environment could cause only minor deflections from a developmental path which was determined in advance by heredity. This view involves what Hunt (1973, p. 9) referred to as belief in "predetermined development". However, even prior to the second world war, evidence was beginning to accumulate that development is far from predetermined. The evidence was most frequently associated with drastic changes in the intellectual performance of children who experienced marked changes in the conditions under which they lived (e.g., Skeels and Dye, 1939). In more recent years, a considerable body of evidence has been developed which shows that learning occurs in even the first few days of life (e.g. Lipsett, 1967), that absence of social intercourse leads to apathy and social retardation in young children (e.g., Dennis, 1960), that deprivation of visual experience in early years as a result of the presence of cataracts leads to permanent deficits in visual capacity (e.g., von Senden, 1960), and so on. This amenability of psychological development to modification as a result of experience involves what Hunt (1973, p. 8) called "developmental plasticity".

Evidence for the existence of developmental plasticity is now very strong. Furthermore, it is apparent that plasticity extends over a very wide range of psychological functions. For example, Greenberg, Uzgaris and Hunt (1968) showed that the ability to co-ordinate seeing and grasping functions, in which infants reach out and grasp an object on which they have focussed their visual attention, is modified by the degree of prior experience in such seeing-and-grasping activities. The use of such sensory-motor functions is greatly facilitated by what might be called "practice". Hunt and his colleagues have also shown that a more clearly psychological, but very basic, cognitive capacity, namely comprehension by the child that an external object exists even when it cannot be seen, is related to living in an environment which offers opportunities for acquisition of cognitive skill. Other aspects of psychological life which have been reported to be affected by experience include the capacity to form social attachments (e.g., Schaeffer, 1964),

the ability to make judgements of depth and to recognize shapes
(e.g., Hudson, 1960; Walk and Gibson, 1961), motivation to seek
pleasure and avoid pain, to receive approval from authorities
or to influence the behaviour of others (e.g., Kagan, 1964),
the presence or absence of "cognitive strain" in situations involving making of decision, facing of conflict and so on (e.g.,
Sarbin, 1968), impulsivity (e.g., Hess and Shipman, 1965), cognitive styles (e.g., Freeberg and Payne, 1967), and so on.

The question of how long the state of plasticity continues
is one of crucial importance for the theory of lifelong education. A second and closely-related key issue is that of the
degree of plasticity that persists at any given age by comparison with the maximum amount of plasticity which ever existed.
Koestler (1964) has argued that the whole process of development from the moment of conception may be conceived of as a
process of decreasing plasticity, with the greatest plasticity
present at the moment of conception, and with all subsequent
experiences and adaptations involving loss of plasticity. Nonetheless, Hunt (1973) has concluded that plasticity continues
throughout life, and that it is present even in the elderly.

*Plasticity, critical periods and interaction*

Plasticity is, of course, a key concept in education. If
predetermined development were truly the case, there would seem
to be little point in discussing how education should be organized. For the purposes of schooling, what is needed is an
understanding of the existence of plasticity and the effect of
increasing age on plasticity. A concept of key importance in
this context is that of "critical periods". Although the whole
area of critical periods is one that has been subjected to a
good deal of psychological debate, and although several conceptualizations of the critical period exist, the main notion can
be fairly simply stated. In a nutshell, belief in the existence of critical periods holds that there are certain age levels at which certain kinds of experience will have the maximum
effects on developing children. It is a matter of some debate
whether experience outside the critical age limits merely has a
reduced effect, or whether effects are minimal or near-zero if
the key experiences occur outside the optimal age limits. Belief in the existence of a large number of critical periods
somewhere within the ages of conventional schooling has probably been one of the articles of faith which has been implicit
in current educational organization.

Indeed, there are strong grounds for believing that, at

the very least, a phenomenon involving something like critical
periods can be seen in human psychological development. Setting aside a considerable body of research with rats, dogs and
monkeys, there are still strong grounds for believing that such
diverse activities in human beings as recognition of shapes and
forms, and judgement of depth, ability to form warm affectional
relationships with other people, and preference for certain cognitive styles are all time-linked. Although it is not universally accepted that critical periods in the classical sense exist, it is clear that the absence of appropriate experiences at
earlier ages leads, for example, in the domains just mentioned,
to permanent and irreversible decrements in behaviour. For example, congenitally blind subjects whose sight was restored after they had been blind since birth showed irreversible defects
in visual perception. Similarly, orphanage-reared children, or
children separated from a mother figure during certain key periods in the first year of life showed permanent decrements in
their ability to form social relationships (e.g., Ainsworth
1966).

The absence of an appropriate earlier press at about the
right time changes the capacity to profit from further stimulation, possibly even at times in the relatively distant future,
and consequently modifies the course of development. Later
stimulation may have its effects neutralized or reduced because
of the effects (or absence of effects) of appropriate earlier
experiences. In this sense, experience and development are fully interactive, experience modifying development, development
partly controlling the ability of experience to exert an influence.

*Modes of teacher influence*

School is, of course, part of the environment with which a child interacts, and teachers are a major aspect of schooling. What mechanisms make it possible for teachers to influence the behaviour of their pupils? At the simplest level, teachers provide simply the *opportunity* for the exercise of psychological functions. In the classroom setting, the pupil has opportunities for social interaction, for contact with knowledge sources such as textbooks and teaching aids, for contact with a flow of information in the structured form constituted by an organized curriculum, and so on. Indeed, mere exercise of psychological functions seems to be of considerable importance to their further development, as research on the decrements in later functions following inhibition of earlier functioning has shown.

Teachers also exercise a much more direct influence on development through the provision of differing *patterns of reward and punishment* in response to different kinds of pupil behaviour. This is not merely a matter of "stamping in" specific responses by rewarding their occurrence and/or punishing their non-occurrence. For example, teachers can reward bold, innovative behaviour or punish it. They can administer a pattern of rewards and punishments that develops the habit of seeking alternative, novel solutions, or they can inhibit it and foster obedience to established authorities such as the textbook. Thus the teacher can, in fact, establish a "*climate*" in which certain attitudes and behaviours are fostered, others suppressed.

An important factor in teachers' influence on children concerns their role as a *model*. Bandura and his associates, for example (e.g., Bandura & Walters, 1963) have shown that children learn patterns of behaviour through the imitation of prestigeous models with whom they come into contact. Consequently, it is important that teachers recognize the importance of their own behaviour as a source of information for pupils about what they should be like. In a sense, this model function of the teacher pervades all other functions. For example, the teacher who insists on exact reproduction of a given text is not only punishing certain kinds of behaviour and rewarding others, is not only establishing a certain motivational and affective climate, but is acting as a model of a particular kind of problem-solving/learning behaviour. However, teachers should not become so concerned about their function as models that they become stilted and artificial in their behaviour -- this too involves provision of a certain kind of model.

*Importance of non-cognitive and non-school factors*

Despite evidence of plasticity, discussion of the ways through which teachers influence pupil behaviour, and so on, recent research has raised serious doubts as to whether or not schools have much influence on their pupils at all. Findings such as those reported by Jencks (1972) in the U.S.A., and the IEA Studies and the Plowden Report in Europe, have suggested that differences between pupils in achievement at school are mainly the result of differences in non-cognitive variables such as motivation for learning, belief in learning as a worthwhile activity, conceptualization of school as a helpful institution, trust or distrust of teachers, and belief that one can actually modify one's fate as a result of schooling. Thus, given a reasonable level of physical facilities and adequate teaching, those children learn most who possess the strongest motivation for learning, the most favourable attitudes towards school, the clearest acceptance of themselves as learners, the strongest acceptance of school as a tool for achieving one's ends, and so on. Consequently, if schooling is to be both more effective and also more capable of meeting the needs of components of society which have not traditionally profited much from it, considerably greater emphasis would seem to be needed in schools on fostering appropriate motivation for learning, self-images, conceptualizations of school, and similar non-cognitive properties.

The second major aspect of the recent findings is that these non-cognitive factors are already strongly-developed in children at the time that they enter school. Furthermore, in present systems of education, they are not much modified by in-school experiences. In other words, the attitudes, motivations and affect which have been shown to be the major sources of differences in school achievement among pupils *are acquired outside school.* These two findings are of great importance here because they emphasize the futility of curriculum organizations which concentrate on cognitive components of learning, and which assume that school can be divorced from the non-school world.

## IMPLICATIONS OF LIFELONG EDUCATION FOR "CURRICULUM"

A key notion in lifelong education is that it will be a process that occurs both in and out of school. Consequently, it is possible to task about "curriculum", in the lifelong education sense, as not only school curriculum, but also out-of-school curriculum. Indeed, life itself is recognized as an

important element of lifelong education, so that one can talk
of a "curriculum" for life, a "curriculum" for work, and so on.
The present section is concerned with the implications of lifelong education for various aspects of this out-of-school curriculum.

*Curriculum for the very young*

If education is to be a lifelong process co-ordinated to
psychological growth at all ages, it will have to be concerned
with very young children.  Indeed, lifelong education recognizes that the early years constitute a stage of psychological
development in their own right, and are not merely a waiting
period prior to later childhood and adolescence, during which
"real" schooling is to take place.  As has been pointed out,
lifelong education recognizes that the early years lay down a
basis on which later psychological development builds.
     This point of view has been strongly stated by Lally
(1972).  He has pointed out that early experience provides an
important base for future learning, whether the developmental
theory applied to the analysis is psychoanalytic, cognitive or
behaviouristic.  Freud, for example, argued that adult personality and motivational structures are based on very early experiences, learning theorists have stressed the resistance of
early learning to subsequent extinction, and both Piaget and
Bruner traced the evolution of adult thinking from early interactions with the environment.  Lally also emphasized the inter-
relationship of emotional, motivational and cognitive processes
in learning, along with the importance of early social experiences.  He concluded that early educative experiences are crucial in laying the groundwork upon which later learning rests.
As a result, children even in the first three years of life
need an appropriate environment that is capable of fostering
cognitive and psychosocial development.
     One practical discussion of what this means for education
is to be found in the "Worth Report" (Worth, 1972), prepared
under the auspices of the government of the Canadian Province
of Alberta.  Worth argues that education should not be denied
to the under-six, and recommends the establishment of formal
systems of early education, which he calls "Early Ed".  He outlines three main goals for Early Ed including provision of stimulation, fostering of a sense of identity, and provision of appropriate socialization experiences (p. 50).  These kinds of
skills do not require formal schooling - they can be fostered
by life itself (Biggs, 1973; Hutt, 1974).  Consequently, a

point which is of great importance for the present purposes,
Worth specifically rejects the notion that early education
should be a downward extension of existing systems. Its main
function would not be the provision of preliminary academic
training in the conventional mould. On the contrary, in advocating early education as the first stage in a system of lifelong education, he suggests that its goal should include developing skills for dealing with information and symbols, promoting
appreciation of various modes of self-expression, nurturing curiosity and ability to think, cultivating children's confidence
in their ability to learn, fostering a sense of self-worth
and finally, increasing the capacity to live with others. In
lifelong education, early psychological growth and associated
educational systems are seen as involving a complex of cognitive, motivational and socio-affective factors which, if appropriately developed, would serve as the basis for a lifetime of
self-fulfilment.

The US National Education Association's Educational Policies Commission (1966) has also discussed in some detail the
need for education in early childhood. They concluded that
early deprivations of desirable developmental and educative experiences have serious effects on later life. In some areas,
later compensatory measures may never be fully effective. Furthermore, exposure to stimulating experiences not only fosters
development, but improves the capacity to profit from later experiences. The report therefore concluded that postponement of
educative experiences until the age of about six is not condu-
cive to optimal development in children. They also pointed out
that this applies to all children, and not only to those traditionally regarded as "deprived" or "disadvantaged". (In the
U.S.A. these labels would refer to, for example, Negroes, the
poor, recent immigrants, and similar groups.) Basically, a
curriculum for the very young should involve "a planned fostering of their development" (1966, p. 4). It should not be viewed as something separate from schooling, but as an essential
part of an integrated system of schooling (i.e., lifelong education).

The report goes on to outline the main features of curriculum for young children. The authors see it as involving four
major areas consisting of not only intellectual, but also emotional, social and physical growth. The goals of this curriculum include the promotion of curiosity, the fostering of language growth, and the development of intellectual tactics for
organizing and reflecting upon experience. These skills are
considered by them as especially important in the light of rapid change in life. It is also of considerable interest to note

E

that they recognize, implicitly if not explicitly, not only the significance of vertical integration of educational systems (as can be seen from their emphasis on the integrated nature of school and very early curricula), but also of horizontal integration of learning. For example, they emphasize the need for provision of educative inputs through many media including television, radio, newsprint, books, records, and so on.

More recently, two other reviews (Eggleston, 1974; Röman, 1974) have outlined some of the main features of curriculum for the very young within a lifelong education orientation. According to Eggleston, the key skill to be fostered is that of language. It is language, for example, that enables people to organize and transmit their own ideas, wishes, thoughts and feelings. Mastery of language permits a giant step towards achievement of self-directedness and consequent reduction of other-directedness. Eggleston also emphasized the importance of early learning experiences for the acquisition of values, thus recognizing the horizontal integration of psychological functioning. Röman, too, stressed the importance of language development among the very young. Other knowledge-oriented factors he emphasized include development of readiness for mathematics and reading skills, diagnosis and remediation of incipient learning difficulties, and the development of problem-solving capacities, a necessary skill if self-directed, independent learning is to be achieved. He extended the curriculum for the very young into the social domain by stressing the need for early mastery of the capacity to communicate, and mastery of a spirit of co-operation with other people. Finally, he drew attention to the importance of the self, stressing the need for a curriculum that includes not only physical fitness, but also fostering of the capacity for self-expression through modes other than the verbal, such as art or calisthenics.

*Curriculum for people beyond conventional school age*

Formal efforts to engage adults in further learning have often failed, especially among those with little prior formal schooling. A frequently-cited reason for this has been, in effect, that the available formal opportunities have not been organized in such a way as to foster lifelong learning among adults. A summary of some of these problems, and some guidelines for developing a lifelong education curriculum for adults is to be found in a paper by Olford (1972). He suggested that such a curriculum should:

1. provide opportunity for students to *initiate* inquiry

2. provide opportunity for students to exhibit creativity and to accept personal responsibility for it
3. provide opportunity for judging of students' work according to their own individual progress
4. provide opportunity for idiosyncratic specialization
5. provide opportunity for development and recognition of a greater diversity of talent.

This outline has been extended by Schaie (1974) who has pointed out the need for a curriculum for adults that takes account of the "rustiness" they experience, or as he put it, aims "to reverse the cultural and technological obsolescence of the aged" (p. 805). One measure he recommends for achieving this goal is the provision of opportunities for the old and the young to interact in their learning experiences by learning together.

*Curriculum for work*

At one time, the work place was one of the obvious and most important sites of learning. However, as Suchodolski (1972) has pointed out, scientific and technological growth have made education through vocational experience impossibly inefficient and ineffective. Nowadays, a long and formal period of preparation is needed for entry into high-level jobs, while work opportunities for the completely unskilled are becoming fewer and fewer. Nonetheless, the very factors which have necessitated this lengthy formal preparation (technological and scientific change) are now rendering it obsolete at ever faster rates. What is needed in the face of this state of affairs is a "curriculum" for the world of work that will foster "personal initiative" (Dubin, 1974) for continued growth and development. Margulies and Raia (1967), for example, showed that this initiative for growth is fostered by supervisory behaviour that openly encourages professional upgrading and development, and by tangible rewards for updating oneself. Dubin (1974, p. 19) has stressed the importance in a work curriculum oriented towards lifelong education, of additional factors, including:
1. provision of tools for self-assessment
2. opportunities for self-assessment
3. establishment of an organizational climate fostering creativity
4. contact with challenging work projects that promote on-the-job solutions to problems
5. peer interactions promoting the exchange of ideas and information

*Curriculum for life itself*

The view that education is essentially something that happens in school is of recent origin. Suchodolski (1972) has traced the rise of the notion that education requires a special environment which is quite distinct from everyday life, and which centres on schools. These schools were "good, difficult and required many years of attendance" (p. 142). Even reforms aimed at democratizing schools retained this basic idea, and concentrated merely upon provision of equal access. As a result, the idea that people can learn through life itself disappeared. Scientific and technological growth made it impossible in the work world, social complexity ruled out education through participation in the life of the society, and so on. As a result, people now live dangerously isolated lives (De'Ath, 1976; Suchodolski, 1976), with a serious risk of "psychic illnesses" (Suchodolski, 1976, p. 173). What is needed is an education capable of developing in people a serious commitment to living a worthwhile life which will go far beyond being merely a "means of existing" (Suchodolski, 1976, p. 176). To enjoy such a life people need an education for life itself as a result of which they learn to live in the present, to meditate upon life, to enjoy art and culture, and to enjoy their own emotions and feelings (i.e., a life of the spiritual as well as the material).

The emergence of the notion of lifelong education suggests that the chance has again arisen of developing a curriculum for life itself, as a result of which people will learn through "participation in social tasks and activities" (Suchodolski, 1972, p. 145), or through sharing in "the social, cultural and professional life of the age" (p. 146). Such a curriculum should emphasize that education involves more than simply intellectual knowledge -- everything that promotes interest and the need to know is important. Clearer recognition of this is a major element in the theory of lifelong education. It would involve both the idea that life itself is a major source of learning, and the view that one can learn about life, mainly through the process of living. Key properties have been summarized by Suchodolski (1972, p. 149) in the following list. A life curriculum will need:

1. To teach people to apply thought to life itself
2. To teach people to want to use knowledge in life
3. To teach people how to use knowledge in life itself
4. To help people to know how to think when in contact with others
5. To help people to know how to exchange social and

cultural experiences with others
6. To teach people how to think, not only in terms of the
rules of science, but also in terms of the requirements
of life itself

## SCHOOL CURRICULUM IN A LIFELONG EDUCATION SETTING

*Survival of schooling*

Lifelong education conceptualizes development, change and
learning as occurring throughout life, not just during a few
years of formal schooling. Consequently, the question arises
whether schooling, as it is currently understood, would survive
in a lifelong education-oriented system. Indeed, some writers
in the area advocate abolition of schooling. Others argue for
a total reorganization, in which the distinction between schooling and living would disappear. Still others conceptualize a
situation in which it would be impossible to talk about a specific period of formal schooling, since schooling would be dis-
tributed throughout life. However, at a practical level, it is
difficult to envisage the sudden disappearance of schooling as
we currently know it. What seems to be a far more likely prospect is that formal schooling will survive, at least in the
short term, even if lifelong education gains widespread acceptance. Agoston (1975), for example, has flatly rejected the
notion that school would wither away with the acceptance of
lifelong education. On the contrary, he argues that, even if
lifelong education were implemented, schools would continue to
play a prominent role. This point of view has been supported
by Hiemstra (1974) who concluded that, in a lifelong education
system, "schools do not become irrelevant and professional
school teachers do not become outmoded".

However, acceptance of lifelong education would probably
involve drastic curricular changes in schools. According to
Delker (1974) they will need to offer an effective core education, so that pupils will be able to acquire the knowledge and
skills needed for a lifetime of learning. They will also have
to offer multiple learning opportunities, and be closely linked
to learning systems lying outside schools such as the home,
work, social life and leisure. In terms of classroom practice,
lifelong education will involve a shift in emphasis away from
transmission of fixed knowledge to the imparting of fundamental
skills, above all learning to learn (Swedish Ministry of Education, 1972). This is seen as meaning that there will be less
emphasis on specialization in school curriculum, and that general and specialist education will move closer to each other.

It also implies more emphasis on communication skills, on the
mass media and on interacting with peer groups.  Finally, lifelong education will involve more individualized learning, more
individual contacts between teachers and pupils, and more individual and group work through projects, investigations, and the
like.

Skager & Dave (1977) have extended the kinds of statements
just made, and have developed a series of criteria for school
curriculum in the light of lifelong education.  The list below
is based on their summary.

1. School curriculum should regard learning processes
   as continuous, occurring from early childhood to
   late adulthood.
2. School curriculum should be viewed in the context
   of concurrent learning processes going on in the
   home, community, place of work, etc.
3. School curriculum should recognize the importance
   of the essential unity of knowledge and the inter-
   relationship between different subjects of study.
4. School curriculum should recognize that the school
   is one of the chief agencies for providing basic
   education within the framework of lifelong education.
5. School curriculum should emphasize autodidactics,
   including development of readiness for further
   learning and cultivation of learning attitudes appropriate to the needs of a changing society.
6. School curriculum should take into account the need
   for establishing and renewing a progressive value
   system by individuals, so that they can take responsibility for their own continuous growth throughout
   life.

*Curriculum and personal development*

The aim of schooling in a lifelong education-oriented
framework will be to develop people who are capable of functioning under minimal supervision, and are willing and able to
adapt and adjust to a changing world.  Thus, curricula will be
required to foster the development of independence, self-respon-
sibility, self-critical analysis, and flexibility (see, for
example, Brock, 1972 and Kupisciewicz, 1972), i.e. they will
have to be heavily concerned with values, attitudes, motivations, and so on.  As Dumazedier (1972) has pointed out, the
world of rapid change will be fraught with intellectual and
emotional insecurity.  If adults are to find life rich and re-

warding under such circumstances, they will need the capacity
to undertake new ventures, play new social roles, work in new
kinds of job, operate within new organizational frameworks, and
so on, with confidence and interest, not fear and reluctance.
Failure to develop the capacity to deal with such situations
will carry with it the threat that individuality may be over-
whelmed by passivity and alienation. Thus, the curriculum will
have to stimulate sensitivity to problems and innovative skills
(e.g., Coste, 1973; Dumazedier, 1972). It should also foster
decision-making skills, skills in coping with organizational
structures ("bureaucratic skills"), and skill in the communication and reception of ideas (e.g., Coleman, 1972). In Dumazedier's (1972, p. 80) words, the curriculum will need to arouse
in everyone the desire to face the new society without passivity or escapism, "...without being put off by the first encoun-
ter with what is new".

*Cognitive development and lifelong education*

The key cognitive skill fostered by a lifelong education-
oriented curriculum will involve applying "innovatory knowledge"
(Dumazedier, 1972, p. 16). The mere task of acquiring information may well be rendered trivial by advancing communications
technology (Richmond, 1973); what will be important will be understanding and using information (turning it into knowledge).
The student will learn to know (e.g., Hicter, 1972; Kidd, 1972)
through analysis of the tactics and codes of knowledge, rather
than through the acquisition of specific bits of information.
The implications for curriculum of this point of view have been
stated very clearly by Covington (1967). He argued that the
heart of classroom practice should be the fostering of productive thinking: particular disciplines would then serve simply
to provide the concrete materials upon which productive or creative thinking would act. This does not mean that the study of
specific subject areas would vanish, but rather that the unifying element in classroom learning would be the productive thinking processes, rather than the facts of the discipline. A curriculum with this orientation is referred to by Covington as a
"cognitive curriculum".

Such a curriculum would foster a grasp of patterns and
forms of knowledge, so that past learning would serve as a basis for the acquisition of new skills (Zhamin and Kostanian,
1972). This view implies an increasing blurring of the bound-
aries between disciplines as they are currently understood. The
common element linking knowledge together would then be the
structure, methods and style of a discipline, rather than the

content of the laws of the discipline, or even the nature of
the phenomena which it studies. Physics, for example, would be
seen as a particular way of thinking about a set of phenomena,
and the discoveries of physics as the application of innovative
thinking to a specific set of problems, rather than as primarily
a set of findings of factual nature.

## ROLE OF TEACHERS IN LIFELONG EDUCATION

The role of teachers in a lifelong education-oriented curriculum has several major features involving their influence on
the attitudes, on the motivational structures and on the cognitive skills of students. In the attitudinal domain, the lifelong education-facilitating teacher will help pupils to adopt a
creative attitude towards new situations, in order to cope with
them effectively and to experience satisfaction from such coping. In the motivational domain, the teacher's major task will
be to arouse in pupils the desire to face change and novelty in
order to come to grips with them and to profit from them, rather
than to avoid them. Cognitively speaking, the teacher's task
will be to equip pupils with skill in gaining skills, as and
when they are required. This will be achieved through the development of a feel for the structure and methods of knowledge,
and through building an understanding of the sources of information that are available. The teacher's fundamental job will be
to foster students' ability to carry out their own investiga-
tion of knowledge, relating what they learn to their own existing knowledge and future needs, and analyzing and evaluating
their own learning as they go.

### *The teacher as co-learner*

The first implication of the lifelong education model for
teachers is that they themselves will have to be lifelong learners (e.g., Dave, 1973). It will be incumbent on them to act as
models of lifelong learning for students. Furthermore, as
teachers will themselves be living in the same changing society
as that which faces pupils, it will be necessary for them continually to adapt and adjust. Indeed, acceptance of lifelong
education is an example of the kind of adjustment that teachers
will have to make. In short, both teacher and pupil will be
engaged in a programme of lifelong learning so that they will
in fact become "co-learners" (Dave, 1973, p. 44).

# Curriculum Implications

*The teacher as guide and facilitator*

The traditional role of the teacher as a fount of knowledge and bearer of traditional wisdom will change. Rather, the teacher is conceptualized as an "educational consultant" (Council of Europe, 1968, p. 53) or "leader" (Hicter, 1972, p. 309) who will facilitate development for each student. In order to achieve this the teacher will function as a "specialist in learning methods" (Frese, 1972, p. 11), as a "co-ordinator of learning activities" (Dave, 1973, p. 44), as an "orchestrator of learning" (IBE, 1975, p. 15), or as one of a group of "facilitators of learning" (Knowles, 1975, p. 235). The basic role implied by all of these writers is that the teacher will guide and co-ordinate learning, rather than being "a purveyor of facts" (IBE, 1975, p. 15). Teachers will not simply impart knowledge in pre-digested packages that have been selected because they contain precisely what all students need. They will help individual students to diagnose their own learning needs, to judge the adequacy of their resources and of the solutions they propose, and to learn in their own way. They will be advisors and resource persons (almost colleagues) rather than distant and infallible authorities.

*Guidance and technology and the teacher's role*

Conceptualizing the teacher as an advisor and guide implies, among other things, a high level of individualization of education. Writers in the area see this individualization as the result of a combination of sophisticated educational guidance and advanced educational technology. Teachers are conceptualized as experts in educational diagnosis. It is assumed that they will be able to supply to students accurate feedback concerning their capabilities, the degree to which their aspirations are realistic, and so on. Simultaneously, it will be necessary for teachers functioning in this manner to be freed from the multitude of routine tasks that currently consume much of their time. Proponents of lifelong education foresee a situation in which, on the basis of accurate assessment procedures, highly individualized programmes will be designed for each student. The capacity of the system to permit students to follow such individualized programmes will be enhanced by educational technology. For example, not only are automated remedial measures and review facilities conceptualized, but also complex, inter-related information systems utilizing devices like teletype terminals connected to remote computerized information

F

facilities.  Even writers who criticize the role of technology
as leading to a crisis state in education seem to see the cause
of the problem (advancing technology) as also offering a way to
overcome it through advanced educational technologies.

*Broadened conceptualization of the teacher*

Discussion to this point has focussed on the implications
of lifelong education for professional teachers, persons specifically trained to teach, and paid to work as teachers as their
principal occupation.  However, one of the most important implications of lifelong education is that, not only will the roles
and skills of professional teachers be expected to change, but
that the idea of just who is a teacher will be greatly expanded
(UNESCO, 1976).  For example, there is already a large group of
what might be called "professional educators" who are, nonetheless, not formally recognized as professional teachers and who
do not function in conventional (school) systems.  This group
of people includes librarians, professional people in zoos,
museums and similar institutions (ornithologists, archaeolo-
gists and the like), education officers in professional associations, training officers in factories or the armed forces, social workers, guidance and family counsellors, and many more.
Increasingly professionals such as doctors, dentists, pharma-
cists, and those in similar occupations, are also coming to be
included in this group, as their professions are more and more
recognized as having preventive and educative functions as well
as curative and restorative.  A second major group of often-un-
recognized teachers contains people who have no formal or professional educative function at all, but do play an important
role as part of the educative functions of life itself.  These
are the people who possess valuable information because they
know how to do things which are important in life -- they are
"practitioners" (UNESCO, 1976, p. 3).  Such people, who might
be called "life educators", include parents, workmates, peers,
social acquaintances, and the like.  It is very important that
the teaching function of this group should not be overlooked.
For many reasons, these last two kinds of teachers (professional educators and life educators) are becoming increasingly important.  For example, young people are demanding experiences in the social milieu of their own societies or abroad,
and in the world of work, not after their education has been
completed but while it is still in progress.  At the same time,
some educational programmes, especially in developing countries,
call for educational activities and services which cannot be

supplied by professional teachers alone. Examples would be
seen in the universal literacy, health and nutrition campaigns
mounted in Tanzania in recent years (Hinzen and Hundsdörfer,
1977). Professional educators and life educators also have the
potential to communicate to students the real "feel" or atmo-
sphere of the world outside the classroom, for example by sharing with them their practical knowledge of the day-to-day reality of being a doctor, a technician or a tradesman. Factors
such as these and others have made it necessary to recognize
and make use of the potential contributions of persons possessing either special professional training or special practical
experience as non-professional teachers.

The result is the emergence, especially within the context
of lifelong education, of a new conceptualization of what constitutes a teacher, or perhaps "educator" would be a better
term, since the word "teacher" is overwhelmingly associated
with formal schooling. These educators, in a system guided by
the principles of lifelong education, would include people with
special technical, manual or artistic skills, physical educators highly skilled in mime, dance and similar activities, people with skill in oral expression or other forms of communication such as drama, and other information specialists such as
journalists, cinematographers, photographers, computer specialists, film producers, and many more (UNESCO, 1976).

Finally, contacts between students and teachers need not
even occur within the confines of schools. For example, the
radio station, the workshop, the theatre, the cinema, the news-
paper office, the union headquarters, the community centre, and
the gymnasium would all function as "classrooms" as well as
places of work. Indeed, it might not even be necessary for students to visit these locations, or even to have face-to-face
contacts with such teachers, since films, videotapes, slides,
audiotapes, computer terminals, even letters and correspondence
courses, would all have the capacity to free teacher-student
contacts from the physical confines of school buildings, and
even the temporal confines of being in the same place at the
same time.

## CLASSROOM IMPLICATIONS OF LIFELONG EDUCATION

*Educational ideals versus classroom practice*

There is a considerable gap between the promulgation and
even widespread acceptance of an abstract, idealized educational principle and the actual day-to-day classroom activities
which represent the practical manifestation of the principle.

This process of "filtering down" of the lofty sentiments into
the actual arena of the classroom can, for convenience sake, be
conceptualized as involving four stages. The first stage cov-
ers the development of the principle as a guiding ideal or goal.
Examples of such idealized goals include "education for democracy", "education for good citizenship", and, of course, "lifelong education". At this level, formulation of the principles
will normally involve analysis of social needs, criticism of
existing systems, philosophical and socio-political statements
about what the ideal human being is like, and so on. The principle being proposed is then normally argued in relatively abstract and lofty terms to meet the needs and defects which have
just been outlined. The first chapters of the present text introduced the concept of lifelong education in this way. Formal
curricula developed and adopted by school systems normally contain some elements of this level of analysis in sections labelled "goals" or some similar heading.

The second step for the purposes of the present analysis
is specification of the implications of the abstract principle
for the philosophy of the curriculum, the role of the teacher,
and so on. However, these statements are usually still broad,
general, and abstract. The recommendations are still in the
form of ideals to be striven for, and not in the form of actual
behaviours to be implemented by teachers in their classrooms.
The analysis of the implications of the concept of lifelong education contained in the sections immediately preceding the
present one is an example of this level of analysis.

The third and fourth steps are less idealistic, less abstract and nearer what actually goes on in a classroom. The
third requires analysis of the implications of the new principle for the kinds of thing that teachers and students actually
do in the classroom. For example, it involves statements about
what sorts of material might be introduced into lessons, what
kinds of activity students ought to participate in, how students' work should be evaluated, and so on. The fourth step in
turning an educational ideal into a living curriculum, requires
specification, not of goals to strive for, but of actual procedures. In formal curriculum documents this step is frequently
accomplished by actual examples, specification of texts to be
used, development of libraries of supportive materials, outlines of just what students ought to know or be able to do at
various points during the school year, and so on.

This fourth step lies beyond the scope of the present text.
Indeed, it would be difficult for any single volume to carry it
out, because the exact nature of the classroom activities which
give expression to a curriculum principle would be expected to

differ markedly from society to society.  Thus, schools in Socialist countries might well actualize abstract principles
through classroom procedures different from those in a Capitalist society.  Again, Third-World classrooms might give expression to an abstract ideal through different day-to-day activities than would be seen in classrooms in a technologically-advanced society, whether Socialist or Capitalist.  However, the
prescriptions concerning curriculum can readily be carried one
step further, even in an essentially abstract and general text
such as the present one.  This is the purpose of the following
paragraphs.  The recommendations and specifications which follow are clearly still generalized and abstract.  Turning them
into concrete classroom behaviours (i.e., carrying out the
fourth step) remains the task of applied curriculum-developers
in the wide variety of societies for which it is claimed lifelong education is a desirable principle to follow.

    Although writing in the context of education in the face
of rapid change rather than specifically about lifelong education, Biggs (1973) has made an analysis of curriculum that is
of interest to the present section.  He distinguished between
"content" learning (learning of selected facts chosen because
they are believed to be valuable), and "process" learning
(learning that changes the ability of students to cope effectively with their future lives, by increasing their ability to
deal effectively and autonomously with novel situations).  This
latter kind of learning may go on in school or elsewhere, and
it may be consciously fostered by teachers or not.  There is,
in fact, an "explicit" curriculum and an "implicit" one.  According to Biggs, learning to cope with change (i.e., process learning) requires (pp. 230-233):
    1. Possessing or being able to locate information.
    2. Possessing highly generalizable cognitive skills.
    3. Possessing general strategies for problem-solving.
    4. Setting one's own objectives.
    5. Evaluating the results of one's own learning.
    6. Being appropriately motivated.
    7. Possessing an appropriate self-concept.
    The first three of these conditions involve what have been
called "cognitive" (or knowledge-oriented) skills in the present text.  The remaining four are concerned with attitudes, motives, values and emotions.  Biggs has acknowledged quite clearly that the state of preparedness for dealing with change involves not merely the cognitive aspects of schooling (i.e.,
transmission of necessary information), but also development
of appropriate socio-affective states.  In doing so, he has,
without making specific reference to it, emphasized the neces-

sity for a curriculum which is horizontally integrated.  He has
then indicated the implications of the personal needs (points
4-7) for curriculum, if people are to be equipped by their
schooling to cope effectively with change.  The implications
he discerned are listed in Table 3, which has been adapted from
the original Biggs paper (1973, p. 237).


TABLE 3

Characteristics of a curriculum for coping with change

| Aspect of Curriculum | Characteristic |
| --- | --- |
| Orientation in time | Oriented towards coping in the future |
| Explicit objectives of learning | Expressive<br>Determined by learners themselves<br>Initially vague, becoming precise as learning progresses |
| Evaluation | Internalized: Learners reflect upon their own performance and provide their own formative evaluation |
| Motivation | Mainly intrinsic<br>Extrinsic motivation may be used to lead the horse to water, but... |
| The implicit curriculum (in very general terms) | Learners will eventually be capable of making their own decisions.  The future is unknown, but it is a challenge they can meet. |

*A three-dimensional analysis of curriculum*

In order to indicate more specifically what adoption of
lifelong education would mean for classroom practice, a three-
dimensional analysis of curriculum is required. The first dimension involves *areas of classroom activity*. This dimension
is conceptualized for the present purposes in terms based upon
Bloom's (1956) analysis of curriculum in his *Taxonomy*. Four
areas of classroom activity have been selected from the list developed by Bloom and his co-workers, for present purposes.
1. Teaching and Learning Methods and Materials,  2. Teacher Activities,  3. Pupil Activities,  4. Evaluation. The second dimension in terms of which the curricular implications of the
concept of lifelong education will be specified involves the
*psychological domain*. Three areas of psychological functioning
will be utilized in the present analysis. These are as follows:
1. Cognitive functions,  2. Motivational systems,  3. Socio-
affective variables. This three-dimensional analysis has been
adopted to maintain the basic psychological approach followed
throughout the text -- analysis in terms of cognition, motivation and affect. The third dimension employed in the present
analysis of classroom implications is the *concept of lifelong
education itself*. The major theoretical implications of lifelong education for school and non-school learning centre on the
concepts of horizontal integration and vertical integration.
For this reason the third dimension of the present analysis involves two levels -- 1. Horizontal integration,  2. Vertical
integration.

Detailed specification of actual classroom activities lies
beyond the scope of the present text. However, it is possible
to indicate fairly specific and relatively precise goals for
curriculum in such a way that the specifications can be turned
into actual classroom behaviours by teachers. Thus, what is
required is to state generalized goals, but in terms that refer
to what actually goes on in the classroom. This will be done
in terms of the three-dimensional model just outlined. A goal
or ideal of lifelong education will be specified by defining
the area of classroom activity involved (e.g., teaching and
learning methods and materials, teacher activities, pupil activ-
ies or evaluation), by specifying the psychological domain concerned (e.g., cognitive functioning, motivational structures,
or socio-affective factors), and finally by specifying the
particular aspect of lifelong learning involved (e.g., vertical
integration or horizontal integration). A particular curricular goal might, thus, be specified as pertaining to fostering
the horizontal integration of cognitive functions through the

kinds of pupil activities involved, and so on.

Specification of curricular goals in this way has been achieved by constructing the four tables which follow. Table 4 is concerned with the first aspect of curriculum defined by Bloom (teaching and learning methods and materials). It is sub- divided to deal separately with the three kinds of psychological functions employed in the analysis, and further subdivided into discussion of the two aspects of lifelong learning already de- fined. Table 5 has a similar organization, involving the same psychological domains and the same aspects of lifelong learning, but dealing with the second aspect of curriculum (teacher activ- ities). Similarly, Tables 6 and 7 follow this framework, but deal with pupil activities and evaluation, respectively. The entries in the tables are statements of a goal for the class- room in the particular area defined by the three-dimensional analysis. These statements are not operational instructions specifying in concrete terms actual activities, but are ideals indicating what goals should be sought in the various areas. Turning these goals into actual teacher and student behaviours is a matter for local design, as has already been pointed out.

Division of the classroom process into these distinct do- mains should not be taken as implying that it is fragmented in this way, in real life. It has already been emphasized that such divisions are made for explanatory purposes only. Similar- ly, the recommendations contained in the four tables are clear- ly by no means exhaustive. Teachers will have little difficul- ty in thinking of other possible entries for these tables. The suggestions actually made here are intended to indicate the general "flavour" of lifelong education-oriented classroom prac- tice and to serve as a jumping-off point for curriculum planners and classroom teachers interested in organizing schools in life- long education terms. The purpose of the suggestions, then, is to be illustrative and, it is hoped, seminal.

TABLE 4

Classroom Goals in the Area of Teaching
and Learning Methods and Materials

| | Lifelong Education Characteristics | |
|---|---|---|
| Psychological Domain | Horizontal Integration | Vertical Integration |
| Cognition | 1. Knowledge presented as a set of techniques for handling problems in life.<br>2. All knowledge interrelated.<br>3. Knowledge can be obtained in the non-school world.<br>4. Examples are drawn from real life.<br>5. Projects and exercises are based on real life. | 1. Unity of learning across age levels is stressed.<br>2. Information introduced in age-appropriate ways.<br>3. Present knowledge seen as the basis of future knowledge.<br>4. Present knowledge seen as outcome of the past. |
| Motivation | 1. Learning seen as desirable goal in itself.<br>2. Self-energized learning is fostered.<br>3. Life aspirations are related to the role of school.<br>4. Desire is established to use school techniques in real life, and vice-versa.<br>5. Expectations of success foster motivation. | 1. Desire for further learning is fostered.<br>2. Expectation of future success leads to continued motivation for learning.<br>3. Prospect of change induces increased motivation.<br>4. Materials produced in the past are used to motivate new learning.<br>5. Methods and materials motivate ongoing |

Table 4 (<u>cont.</u>)

| Psychological Domain | Lifelong Education Characteristics | |
| --- | --- | --- |
| | Horizontal Integration | Vertical Integration |
| Motivation (Cont'd) | 6. Expectations of utility of learned material foster learning. | learning. |
| Affect | 1. Knowledge seen as a tool for coping with life. | 1. Pupils define themselves as continuing learners. |
| | 2. Learning is seen as a logical technique for solving life problems. | 2. Learning thought of as an appropriate preparation for the future. |
| | 3. Confident attitudes to oneself as a learner are established. | 3. Learning is seen as a tool with continuing use. |
| | 4. The self is seen as part of a network of learning. | 4. Change defined as interesting and a challenge. |
| | 5. School is defined as *one* source of information linked with others. | 5. Sense of confidence in self as competent to face the future is fostered. |

TABLE 5

Classroom Goals in the Area of Teacher Activities

| Psychological Domain | Lifelong Education Characteristics | |
|---|---|---|
| | Horizontal Integration | Vertical Integration |
| Cognition | 1. Teacher is co-ordinator of knowledge. | 1. Teacher refers back and ahead in presenting material. |
| | 2. Teacher provides guidance on sources of information. | 2. Teacher stresses increasing ease of problem-solving with new learning. |
| | 3. Teacher "inter-learns" with students. | |
| | 4. Teacher "models" lifelong learning. | 3. Teacher stresses advances with new knowledge and supplementing of old. |
| | 5. Teacher emphasizes links between school learning and real-life effectiveness. | 4. Teacher displays knowledge of the past. |
| | 6. Teacher draws on non-school experiences. | 5. Teacher discusses the world of the future in class. |
| | 7. Teacher draws on non-school information. | 6. Teacher emphasizes keeping up to date. |
| | 8. Teacher draws exemplary material from real life. | |
| Motivation | 1. Teacher energizes self-directed learning. | 1. Teacher rewards use of new learning to solve problems |
| | 2. Teacher rewards cross-application of knowledge. | 2. Unsolved problems temporarily deferred pending new learning. |
| | 3. Teacher fosters introduction of non-school issues and materials. | 3. Teacher also seeks new learning. |

Table 5 (<u>cont</u>.)

| Psychological Domain | Lifelong Education Characteristics | |
|---|---|---|
| | Horizontal Integration | Vertical Integration |
| Motivation (Cont'd) | 4. Teacher rewards attempts to apply school knowledge to real-life situations.<br>5. Teacher encourages the participation of parents and other elements of the community in schooling. | 4. Teachers reveal their own desire for change.<br>5. Teachers reward and encourage planning for future. |
| Affect | 1. Teacher defines self as member of broad learning network including non-school world.<br>2. Teacher adapts collegial attitudes to students.<br>3. Teacher downgrades image of self as possessor of exclusive information and sole source of knowledge. | 1. Teacher defines self as continuing learner.<br>2. Teacher presents learning as way of developing oneself.<br>3. Teacher allays anxiety about future.<br>4. Teacher fosters confidence in pupils' own ability to continue learning. |

TABLE 6

Classroom Goals in the Area of Pupil Activities

| Psychological Domain | Lifelong Education Characteristics | |
| --- | --- | --- |
| | Horizontal Integration | Vertical Integration |
| Cognition | 1. Pupils apply knowledge of one discipline to others. | 1. Pupils utilize earlier learning as basis for present. |
| | 2. Pupils apply methods of one discipline to others. | 2. Pupils see present learning as the basis of future learning. |
| | 3. Pupils recognize tactics of disciplines and see common ground. | 3. Pupils analyze relationship of past learning to present problems. |
| | 4. Pupils apply school-based skills to non-school issues. | |
| | 5. Pupils introduce examples and materials from non-school world. | 4. Pupils act as sources of information for younger and seek information from other. |
| | 6. Pupils show familiarity with differing sources of knowledge. | 5. Pupils plan learning with future in mind. |
| Motivation | 1. Pupils seek new learning. | 1. Pupils seek new learning when confronted with problems for which present knowledge is inadequate. |
| | 2. Pupils experience satisfaction and reward in learning. | |
| | 3. Pupils show willingness to apply knowledge to non-school world. | 2. Pupils experience satisfaction when old problems solved by present learning. |
| | 4. Pupils seek to find innovative and cross-disciplinary solutions to problems | |

Table 6 (<u>cont.</u>)

| Psychological Domain | Lifelong Education Characteristics | |
|---|---|---|
| | Horizontal Integration | Vertical Integration |
| Motivation (Cont'd) | 5. Pupils show willingness to assume roles as leader, "tutor" of fellows, and so on. | 3. Pupils actively seek opportunities for continuous learning. |
| Affect | 1. Pupils treat learning as a general tool for problem-solving. | 1. Pupils show understanding of learning as a tool of future self-development. |
| | 2. Pupils define school as part of a learning network. | 2. Pupils see the inadequacy of present knowledge as a solution for all future problems. |
| | 3. Pupils define selves as part of a learning network. | |
| | 4. Pupils regard knowledge as a single fabric. | 3. Pupils define selves as capable of change in social roles. |
| | 5. Pupils define selves as leaders and innovators, as well as followers. | 4. Pupils plan for future learning. |

TABLE 7

Classroom Goals in the Area of Evaluation

| Psychological Domain | Lifelong Education Characteristics | |
| --- | --- | --- |
| | Horizontal Integration | Vertical Integration |
| Cognition | 1. Positive credit is given for recognizing cross-linkages in knowledge. | 1. Evaluation diagnoses past deficiencies and implies remedial action. |
| | 2. Evaluative procedures emphasize application of knowledge to solving of problems. | 2. Evaluation indicates the adequacy of present as a basis for future learning. |
| | 3. Evaluation functions as information or feedback to pinpoint deficiencies in knowledge, not as means of sorting pupils. | 3. Evaluation provides a jumping-off point for new learning, re-evaluation, etc., not an end in itself. |
| | 4. Credit given for non-school activities. | 4. Evaluation is basis of planning future learning. |
| Motivation | 1. Evaluation rewards application of school skills to real life. | 1. Evaluation fosters a desire for future learning. |
| | 2. Evaluation rewards application of non-school skills to classroom. | 2. Evaluation sets up reasonable expectations for the future. |
| | 3. Evaluation procedures are used to foster self-assessment. | 3. Evaluation establishes expectations of future success. |
| | 4. Evaluation is used to motivate new learning. | 4. Evaluation leads to the establishment of realizable goals. |
| | 5. Evaluation helps to foster realistic levels of aspiration. | |

Table 7 (<u>cont.</u>)

| Psychological Domain | Lifelong Education Characteristics | |
| --- | --- | --- |
| | Horizontal Integration | Vertical Integration |
| Affect | 1. Evaluation emphasizes clearer understanding of self and capacities.<br>2. Evaluation fosters self-image of competence in many areas.<br>3. Evaluation provides guidance concerning pupils' inter-relationships with real world.<br>4. Evaluation integrates non-school information.<br>5. Evaluation integrates non-school people (e.g. parents). | 1. Evaluation provides a reasonable picture of how self may develop in the future.<br>2. Evaluation establishes a feeling of confidence in own ability to cope with the future.<br>3. Evaluation establishes a self-image as person capable of coping through learning. |

# Chapter 8

# Criticisms and Future Prospects

The present chapter reviews some of the criticisms of life-long education as a principle for the organization of schooling, and discusses some of the prospects of the future. This task lies outside the strict goals of the text (a psychological analysis of the validity of lifelong education), but it is necessary for an adequate treatment of the topic.

In the sections which follow, critical analyses of life-long education are reviewed in a fairly full way, and an attempt is made to communicate the full force of the criticisms. The purpose of this presentation is not, however, to destroy the credibility of lifelong education, but to find how it can be further developed and improved. For this reason, the critical comments are extended by discussion of the necessary further research, and by review of some of the practical steps which must be taken if a workable principle is to be established and put into practice. A great deal of valuable material may be obtained from criticism, when it is viewed as analysis of the weakest points of the theory, advice concerning what is lacking, feedback on defects in the presentation of the main ideas, and similar information. It is in this positive and constructive sense that the review of criticism is meant to be taken, not as an attempt to invalidate the principle.

## LACK OF NOVELTY

*Old wine in new bottles*

The idea of education and learning as lifelong processes is by no means new. The basic notion is to be seen in writings dating back to antiquity (Asian Institute, 1970). More recently, it has been given prominence by European educational theorists such as Comenius (Kyrasek and Polisensky, 1968) and

149

Matthew Arnold (Johnson, 1972). In modern times, the exact
term "lifelong education" first appeared in English educational
writings about 50 years ago (see Richmond, 1973). The main
ideas of lifelong education in its modern form were spelled out
immediately after the second world war, although in the context
of "further education" rather than "lifelong education" (Jacks,
1946). Nonetheless, no general theory of education as a lifelong process has gained widespread acceptance in English-lan-
guage writing, despite early attempts to develop a unified and
unifying theory in the area. Educational thinkers have continued to conceptualize education as "the influence exercised by
adult generations on the young" as Durkheim (1961) put it. This
definition clearly sees education as something that is done to
children by those who are older and wiser. It also sees education as ending when real "life" begins (Lindeman, 1961). It
persists in the view that Suchodolski (1972) has criticized --
that education and life are somehow separate processes.

        Just like the idea that education can be lifelong, the
idea of education as a factor in the development of healthy personalities is by no means new, nor is the emphasis lifelong education theorists place on learning the structure and form of a
discipline rather than merely its facts. The need to foster
motivation for learning, the role of the teacher as adviser and
co-learner, and many similar points of view that have been associated here with lifelong education, will all be familiar to
students of education. In fact, few of the individual elements
of recent theory of lifelong education are novel. To what extent then is there anything new or innovative about the concept?
Is it simply a matter of placing an old wine into new bottles?


*The unifying role of recent theory*

        A continuing problem for educational theorists has been
that, although there are scattered and fragmentary statements
that emphasize the lifelong nature of educative learning, these
have not been collected and organized into a unified theory of
lifelong education. Thus, although lifelong education is, to
some extent, merely the revival of earlier ideas, it can claim
to represent a novel contribution to educational thinking if it
organizes and systematizes pre-existing ideas and presents them
in a coherent and acceptable form at the right moment in time.
A systematic educational theory is considerably more than the
sum of its individual ideas, just as a chain is considerably
more than just a collection of links. Thus, a theory can have
a novelty that resides, not in the novelty of the individual

elements, but in their juxtaposition and their formal unifica-
tion into a coherent system. To the extent that present statements about lifelong education have achieved this status, they
may claim novelty and value.

Consequently, despite the fact that the individual elements of the theory of lifelong education are, by and large,
all ideas that educational theorists have encountered before
(albeit in scattered and fragmentary form), there is something
new and unique in the concept. Indeed, a little reflection indicates that, among other things, the thorough-going adoption
of lifelong education would result in substantial changes in
the organization and processes of schooling. One of those
changes would be drastically different roles for formal schools
and for teachers. The unique contribution of the concept of
lifelong education has thus been that it organizes and inte-
grates many existing threads or strands of argument into a coherent whole in response to a felt need in contemporary life.
As a result, the implications for real life can now be worked
out in detail. In fact, then, the concept of lifelong education may be said to possess novelty in that it involves a new
whole that is emerging from the fusion of existing but uninte-
grated individual elements.

## LACK OF A RIGOROUS BASIS

*Unnecessary sentimentality*

Discussions of lifelong education are frequently internally inconsistent, juxtaposing for example criticism of the effects of technology on the quality of life with simultaneous
proposals that technology will provide the solution. They also
depend very heavily on what Vinokur (1976) called "nostalgic
idealism" and Elvin (1975) "the modish" (p. 26), or the reflection of "a theological cosmogeny" (p. 26). What is usually
lacking is a systematic analysis of things like the ideological
base of the theory of lifelong education, the feasibility and
practicability of the concept, and related issues. Much of the
writing in the area involves attachment of a whole set of what
may well be unnecessary sentimental ideals that are not inherent
in the concept at all. Many theorists seem to use the label
"lifelong education" as a jumping off point for extolling the
virtues of whatever they think education should be like, according to their own values and ideals. To others it is "a
magic formula" (Elvin, 1975, p. 26), or "a universal panacea"
(Cropley, 1974).

One possible example of this excessive sentimentality is

to be seen in the identification of lifelong education with
humanistic values, goals and ideals.  Certainly writings in the
area are frequently humanistic in orientation, and seem to assume that a system of lifelong education would necessarily be
based on humanistic principles.  It can be argued that such
principles are not necessarily inherent in the concept.  On the
other hand, content analysis of the literature such as that
contained in Dave (1976) certainly suggests that humanistic
principles are part of the definition of lifelong education, by
usage if not by inherent meaning of the term.

### Failure to define key concepts

Possibly as a result of the fact that the meaning of lifelong education is emerging through consensus rather than through
strict definition, much of the literature has been notably ineffective, in that it has failed to specify clearly what is
meant by "learning", and how the two are related, for example
through schooling, in work or in life.  It could be said that
education is already lifelong, if by "education" is meant individual change as a result of contact with educative experiences.  In a similar vein, the literature has been notable for
the infrequency of attempts systematically to explain the relationship between education, schooling, learning, personal and
social development, and school curriculum.  This deficiency has
been recognized in the present text, and attempts have been
made to clarify some of the interactions mentioned.

### Failure to provide empirical evidence

Analyses of lifelong education have seldom made a careful
analysis of the empirical evidence for believing that the kinds
of expedients proposed for reforming education, both in and out
of school, would actually have the desired results.  Indeed, it
is not at all clear whether or not such evidence exists.  Acceptance of many of the pronouncements of proponents of lifelong education looks to be mainly a matter of face validity,
or even shared ideology, rather than of commitment based on
analysis of evidence.  Similarly, there is very little discussion in the literature of the question of how the outcomes of
lifelong education would be evaluated, even if there were specific and specifiable goals for lifelong-oriented procedures.
How would administrators, politicians, or educational theorists
know whether changes had taken place and, more importantly,
whether those changes would be responsive to the kinds of prob-

lem they were supposed to deal with? Some efforts in this direction have been made by the UNESCO Institute in Hamburg,
which has attempted to design and carry out empirical studies
of various aspects of lifelong education and associated curricula.

## FAILURE TO DEAL WITH THE ISSUES

Another criticism of lifelong education is that not only
is it sentimental, idealistic and utopian, but that, in any
case, it ignores the real issues which need to be taken into
account in designing educational reform, even if, to some extent, it correctly identifies the broad problems such as inequity and similar issues.

### *Failure to come to grips with the real problem*

Although it has been argued in other sections that lifelong education involves a radical restructuring of education
in direct response to a felt need (see for example later sections of the present chapter - p. 158), writers such as Dauber,
Fritsch, Liegle, Sachs, Scheilke and Spiekermann (1975) have
taken the opposite view, claiming that it does not strike at
the heart of the real problem. Instead of analyzing, with the
aim of eliminating them, the social conditions which inhibit
the growth of self-directed learning, equal opportunity and the
like, lifelong education simply offers a new form of remedial
or compensatory education. Consequently, it may even be criticized, according to these authors, as being essentially only
a more sophisticated way of adapting people to an inhumane or
exploitive society. However, in assessing the cogency and practical usefulness of these authors' criticisms, it is important
to bear in mind that they stem from a particular political
point of view (Marxism) which requires a particular kind of
analysis of all politico/economic systems, so that the edge of
their criticisms is somewhat blunted. This is also true to
greater or lesser extent of some of the other critics in the
area.

### *Failure to deal adequately with economic issues*

Two broad economic questions also arise in connection with
lifelong education. The first of these can be stated quite
plainly: How is it to be paid for? Presumably, the development

of an all-encompassing, lifelong system of education will en-
tail additional expenditures but, in some countries, especially
less-developed countries in Asia, Africa and Latin America, it
is difficult to find the money to establish even a basic education system along traditional lines. Procedures which threaten
increased expenditures may thus be out of the question. The
second economic problem that has not been adequately analyzed
by proponents of lifelong education is just what priority lifelong education should have in development plans for less-wealthy
countries. The returns from implementation of lifelong education may be primarily social or spiritual, rather than monetary
or material. In many countries, the primary interest of social
planners may center on the production of food and the development of viable economies, rather than on psychic rewards. In
such a context, the call for expenditure in pursuit of such
goals as self-fulfilment may seem absurd. Consequently, the
question arises what kind of cost/benefit analysis should be
carried out (e.g., Elvin, 1975). If practical benefits flow
from lifelong education, for example in the form of some kind
of economic benefits to a society, these need to be dealt with
by theorists in the area. At present most writings ignore
these kinds of issue, or else deal with them by pronouncements,
which often flow from doctrine or faith, rather than from theoretical and empirical analyses.

Finally in the economic domain, lifelong education has
implications for the production and distribution of resources.
However, these implications may be different for different societies at different times (see Elvin, 1975). For example, the
effects of lifelong education, or even the question of whether
it is desirable or not, may be quite different in developing
countries as against technologically-advanced countries characterized by lengthy experience with an industrialized economy.
Again, the implications of lifelong education may differ in
socialist and capitalist societies as a result of the differing
economic structures in the two kinds of society. It is also
possible that lifelong education may be impossible in existing
economic structures, and may require the development of new
kinds: Vinokur (1976) for example has argued that the most widely accepted economic/educational models in capitalist societies
would not permit lifelong education to take place. The "human
resources" model implies that education should occur early in
life, that it should be formally organized, that it should be
scarce, and that it should be costly. Even the "filter model"
sees lifelong education as confined to on-the-job training. Indeed, according to Vinokur, even if lifelong education became a
reality in existing capitalist societies, it would benefit main-

ly workers in the "primary market" (roughly understandable as "the bourgeoisie"), and would result primarily in increased job dissatisfaction for workers in the "secondary market".

However, these latter kinds of criticism lose some of their force when it is borne in mind that they often spring from doctrinaire opposition to the capitalist mode of production or to an excessive fear that lifelong education will be seized upon as a way of increasing worker productivity. Such criticisms often also suffer from a fault for which proponents of lifelong education have been criticized; a naive faith in human nature and an utopian tendency to apply idealistic solutions derived from theory rather than empirical validation. Increased productivity would probably be rejected by most writers as a reason for the adoption of lifelong education. Nonetheless, there seems to be nothing fundamentally wrong with it, provided that it was a result of worker interest, intrinsic motivation, and similar factors, rather than a cause of increased alienation.

In the case of developing nations, lifelong education may not be a luxury or a piece of absurdly unrealistic theorizing at all. It may even offer the best path to the achievement of practical goals such as improvement of the quality of life. The link between education and improved standard of living has already been mentioned in an earlier chapter. Developing countries may have the most to gain from adoption of lifelong education, the greatest need for it, the best opportunity to develop it, and the most fertile ground for its growth. This is because such countries often either lack or have consciously rejected the educational structures and practices of their former colonial powers, so that they lack a thoroughly-entrenched educational establishment and rigid public views on what schools should be like. They may be ripe for innovation. At the same time, many of the principles of lifelong education clearly resemble traditional educational practices in such countries, with their emphasis on the link between educational activities and real life, their use of members of the community as teachers, and similar properties. Thus, lifelong education may not be as great an absurdity for developing countries as might at first seem to be the case. Indeed, an educational reform such as the one adopted in Tanzania in recent years (Hinzen und Hundsdörfer, 1977) has much in common with lifelong education, despite the fact that it was adopted on hard-headed, practical grounds, not naive sentimentalism.

Criticism of lifelong education on the grounds that how it is to be paid for has not been adequately considered often fails to take into account the fact that lifelong education can

be considered in qualitative as well as quantitative terms. For
example, its cost implications may involve not so much a question of increased or reduced expenditures, as one of *changed* expenditures, with the money involved being spent on different
things (e.g., information storage and retrieval services instead of school buildings). Furthermore, the changes in the
quality or kind of educative experiences resulting from the
adoption of the principles of lifelong education may be such
as to foster the feeling that existing monetary allocations are
being better spent, that better value is being obtained for
money. As a result, in cost/benefit terms, economies may be
achieved, without reduction in expenditure, or even in the face
of increased spending.


## LIFELONG EDUCATION AND "THE ESTABLISHMENT"

*Lifelong students and perpetual dependency*

Some writers, and especially those who advocate deschooling, have argued that the learning experiences of the young are
already too bureaucratized and over-organized. To them lifelong education implies an intensive and ubiquitous central planning and control of education, and hence of the development of
the individual (e.g., Dauber et al, 1975). It is true that the
concept of an educational hierarchy whose influence extends
from the cradle to the grave raises the spectre of an educational establishment of awe-inspiring power. One obvious concomi-
tant of lifelong education is lifelong students, condemned to
perpetual inadequacy (Ohliger, 1974). This criticism has been
stated very forcefully by Dauber et al (1975). They point out
that, in a lifelong education society, those who do not learn
continually will rapidly become obsolete or out of date. As a
result it would be necessary for everyone to engage in a fran-
tic process of endless learning, simply to avoid falling be-
hind. The main motivation for learning could thus become fear
of inadequacy, the main result people perpetually dependent
upon the educational system. They have also pointed out that
continual relearning and endless adjustment increases the opportunities for people to experience failure. Furthermore, the
responsibility for such failure will rest squarely on the individual involved, so that a sense of inadequacy may be fostered. Indeed, if lifelong students implies people who spend
their lifetimes in the relatively remote, detached-from-life
and dependent traditional role of students, it may not be something to be welcomed.

This possibility gains credence when it is borne in mind

that, at the present moment, interest in lifelong education is
primarily to be seen in large bureaucratic organizations.  Con-
ferences and discussions on the topic have tended to be confined to high-level civil servants, specialists and experts, and
members of the European educational establishment!  Despite the
emphasis on horizontal integration, with all elements of society and all aspects of life recognized as educative, it is most
noticeable that persons who are not professional educators have
not participated extensively in discussions of lifelong education.  It is difficult to get rid of the feeling that implementation of lifelong education would serve only to extend state
control of human lives by providing a rationale for cradle-to-
grave regimentation.  Indeed, as Illich and Verne (1975) have
pointed out, lifelong education has the potential to develop
into the most perfect instrument for the subjugation of the individual that has yet been devised.


*Vested interests*

     A second problem in this area concerns the existence of an
enormous establishment with a very strong vested interest in
the maintenance of certain elements of the status quo.  At the
heart of the idea of lifelong education is the view that schooling as we know it will be drastically transformed.  However,
the very persons who seem to have the most to lose from such a
development (teachers, teacher-educators and similar personnel)
are those who have the responsibility for developing lifelong
educational systems and for working out the details of the concept's application in real life.  Without attributing ill will
to any of these people, it seems unlikely that an educational
reform of the magnitude implied by the theory of lifelong education will emerge from the deliberations of the educational
mandarins or even from those of the smaller fry.  Many individual teachers and other educational workers may accept the idea
of lifelong education in principle, but its implementation
seems likely to be impeded by the sheer inertia of largescale
bureaucratic structures such as are seen in many educational
systems.  As a result, there is a danger that an excessively
watered-down variant of lifelong education will eventually
emerge in the schools, with the existing systems adjusting to
the new pressures by "rolling with the punches".
     Lifelong education could also serve primarily as a device
for propping up the status quo in other areas of society, rather than as a source of fundamental reform.  It could serve, for
example, primarily to make education more profitable to capital,

by helping to adapt the labour force more rapidly to the changing needs of industry.  If collectively financed, it could
transfer the burden of paying for upgrading and retraining from
the shoulders of industry to those of the individual taxpayer.
In addition, it would guarantee a ready-made market for the
products of the education industry.  Lifelong education also
has the potential to become a device for stifling educational
dissent.  It could do this by providing extended means for
keeping surplus labour docile and under control, and also by
absorbing popular education movements, through incorporating
them into the lifelong education apparatus (see Vinokur, 1976
for an extended discussion).  Thus, it is a potentially danger-
ous idea with great possibilities for misuse.
     The adoption of lifelong education seems, therefore, to
have the potential for turning the whole society into either a
giant factory or a perpetual school.  Thus, the critical question must be faced whether lifelong education is to function
as a means of enslaving society, or of freeing it.  The emphasis placed by proponents of lifelong education on self-directed learning, self-evaluation, self-fulfilment, improved
quality of life, and similar factors indicates that its principles tend in the direction of independence, variety of experience and autonomy, rather than in that of confinement within a self-perpetuating socio-economic system.  It is, in fact,
very important to remember that lifelong education is not conceptualized as simply something to make people more productive,
and better employees.  Although the acquisition of technical
and vocational knowledge cannot be ignored, lifelong education
is concerned with cultural experiences and personal development;
it is concerned with freeing people (Suchodolski, 1976).


## UTOPIANISM

*Lifelong education as a radical concept*

     Although the claims of lifelong education are currently
being advanced mainly by large organizations of national or
international character, its implementation would, as has been
pointed out, result in educational changes of extraordinary
breadth, and possibly in the near-disappearance of educational
structures as we currently know them.  Thus, at least as a theoretical formulation, the concept of lifelong education is of
sufficiently sweeping nature to justify calling it a "radical"
theory.  As with many radical proposals that are advanced in a
flush of enthusiasm, its literature abounds with problems arising from the fact that many of its proponents make Utopian

claims for it.

*Idealized model of man*

One theme that is prominent in writings on lifelong education, even if implicitly rather than explicitly, is the view
that all human beings have identical potentials for development.
Many writers seem to assume that all differences in behaviour
that are seen between adults or between children are entirely a
matter of motivation and similar socio/affective variables. Furthermore, it seems to be assumed that these differences are entirely of environmental origin.  At the same time, however,
there is much discussion of techniques for identifying precise
details of each student's psychological functioning, and designing educational regimens that are precisely tailored to the
needs of each individual student.  It is often argued that this
will be done through the development of educational guidance
techniques to heights unknown at present.  Individualization of
programs is often seen as flowing from the application of an
advanced educational technology -- a kind of *deus ex machina*!
Curiously, these kinds of sentiment are sometimes juxtaposed
with comments on the perniciousness of psychological testing
and the alienation flowing from technology.

In fact, much of the literature on lifelong education
rests on a particular model of the nature of man, what Duke
(1976, p. 86) called the " 'optimistic' model of man's potential ".  According to this model, people are basically noble
and good, but are perverted by their teachers and the society
in which they live.  Children are regarded as co-operative,
non-competitive, and non-aggressive by nature, but trained to
act in unnatural ways by the social system in which they are
reared.  Many of the writers in the area assume that a system
organized in terms of lifelong education would not have exams,
classroom tests, or evaluation of any kind.  Motivation, they
claim arises from the natural thirst for knowledge which is
said to be innate in all people.  On the other hand, some writers have strongly emphasized a role for evaluation, but regard
it as serving the purpose of helping develop people who can
cope with technological and social change, can understand themselves and other people, and possess the basic skills of knowledge and communication.  The almost religious fervor of some
writers in this area, especially when their notion of basic
human nature is involved, was emphasized by Musgrave (1975)
when he suggested that believers in original sin would not be
attracted to the idea of lifelong education.

*Role of work*

   Writings on lifelong education frequently assume that vocational preparation will become secondary or disappear as a
goal of education.  Rather, self-fulfillment will become the
chief purpose for which people will be educated.  It is then
suggested that work too will become a means of self-expression
rather than a necessity.  In the absence of a vocational purpose for learning, it is believed that ultimately learning for
its own sake will become the norm, even for the people in the
street.  Learning will be carried on, not for any extrinsic
gains that result from it, but for the "creative joy in partic-
ipating in it" (Bowles, 1971, p. 496).  In contrast to this
conceptualization of a society dominated by intrinsic motivation, joy in participation, self-fulfillment and creativity,
other writers advance the view that society is in danger of
moving towards a world in which people, although well-supplied
with the basic necessities for survival, run the risk of living
"the creative existence of termites" (Aron, 1968).


*Faith in the power of school*

   Discussions of the role of school in fostering intellectual and cognitive skills of a lifelong education-oriented kind,
as well as attitudes, values, and motivations that will stimulate lifelong learning, are based on the assumption that school
exercises an important influence in these areas.  There are,
however, many suggestions that the potency of school is much
less than has previously been thought to be the case (see
Simmons, 1973, for a recent summary).  On the other hand, a
major notion in lifelong education is that school will assume
a relatively minor place in the educative processes that people experience.  Consequently, those aspects of the theory of
lifelong education that minimize the role of school can, perhaps, be said not to be Utopian at all.  However, as has already been pointed out earlier in the present chapter, the question then arises of how realistic it is for well-established,
professional educators to talk about educational systems that
would profoundly change as we presently know it.
   It is not unfair to say that there is a tendency among
writers in the area of lifelong education to hail the concept
as a pattern of educational organization which will usher in
the educational millennium (Cropley, 1974).  Inequality, low
levels of motivation, alienation from school and learning, and
many other problems will, according to this view, all be eliminated.  It is also fair to say that much of the writing about

lifelong education has a particular ideological slant.  In addition, educational theorists have tended to claim for lifelong education virtues in connection with everything that they hold to be educationally good (Knowles, 1975).  As a result, it is necessary to examine the concept with some reservations.  The relatively hard-headed reader is likely to be turned away by the aura of faith and mystique which is beginning to be built around it.

Nonetheless, as the basic concepts in lifelong education are a matter of considerable interest, an attempt should be made to evaluate it independently of any exaggerated claims or of the "politics" of its proponents.  The pace and style of change do seem to be accelerating, so that there seems to be little doubt that education as we know it really is in danger of perpetuating skills and social structures which may well be obsolete in a few years.  Increasing technology really is causing sweeping social changes, and it really is necessary to ask whether present educational systems may not have served their purpose.  Thus, a serious and self-critical analysis of lifelong education is called for.

## FUTURE NEEDS AND PROSPECTS

*Responding constructively to criticism*

Many of the criticisms which have been reviewed in the present chapter suffer themselves from faults attributed to lifelong education.  For example, they are often doctrinaire or utopian.  Such criticisms seem forced and negative or destructive in nature; they may have little practical potential for application to the analysis of lifelong education.  However, many of the other criticisms are clearly well-founded, and need to be considered carefully.  Some of these involve deficiencies which can be fairly readily remedied, or are even in process of being remedied in the most recent writing in the area, such as criticisms that there is insufficient information on a particular point, that details have not been worked out in some areas, or that certain issues have not sufficiently been taken into account.  Others, however, are of more profound nature, and need to be taken very seriously, so that appropriate steps can be taken to deal with the problems they raise.  In particular, it is very important that proponents of lifelong education avoid what has already been called "rolling with the punches", by simply adjusting their pronouncements in such a way as to avoid criticism without actually doing anything about it, in a process of "dynamic conservatism" (Duke, 1976, p. 87).

At this point, two major practical steps seem to be called
for. The first is that the ideas put forward under the heading
"lifelong education" need to be communicated to people in positions lower down the educational hierarchy. This would be a
positive response to the criticism that the idea is presently
confined to the establishment. It would also work in favour of
emergence of lifelong education as a true grassroots reform
movement, rather than as a new device for turning out docile
and passive workers or for stifling educational reform.

In addition to communicating the principle to the public
and especially to the non-school educative agencies in life
which are so much emphasized in writings on lifelong education,
this also requires introduction of the notion into teacher
training. However, it is important that the idea of lifelong
education does not become simply another trend or fad promoted
in teachers colleges but quickly abandoned by young teachers
once they come to grips with the harsh realities of real
schools. There is thus a strong need for teachers in the field
too to be acquainted with the principles of lifelong education,
for example through continued in-service learning on their part,
in a practical example of vertical integration. In addition,
it is very important that supervisory personnel such as school
principals, inspectors and similar people endorse the ideas of
lifelong education, if it is to have any substantial effects
on school practice.

The second major advance in the development of lifelong
education as an educational principle of practical significance
requires its specification in terms directly applicable to real-
life educational activities. At the school level, for example,
this requires the working out of its implications for classroom practice, attempts to put these into effect, and evaluation of the consequences. This process would involve translation of the philosophy or goals of lifelong education into
statements about school curriculum, including determination of
goals in concrete terms understandable even to persons without
strong commitment to lifelong education, specification of teaching and learning activities likely to achieve these goals, development of learning aids, and working out of evaluative procedures and criteria. The ultimate aim would be specification
of what the adoption of lifelong education as an organizing
principle would mean to the classroom teacher, indication of
what kinds of activities would put this goal into effect, development of supportive materials, and design of techniques for as-
certaining what kind of change ultimately resulted.

*Necessary further research*

Achievement of the practical goals just outlined may, however, not yet be possible.  It is still, in much of the writing in the area, basically a philosophy or even a direction of educational development, and not a set of rules or activities. Before such a stage of development of the principle can be achieved, many practical questions need to be answered.  As a result, there is pressing need of a great deal of research of an applied kind in the area, quite apart from abstract and essentially theoretical questions such as that of the meaning of lifelong education, or its psychological basis.

One problem is that educational psychology has tended to concentrate on the ways in which people learn as individuals. Where the effects of others have been taken into account, they have tended to be treated as reinforcers or as providers of cues.  What is needed is an "educational social psychology" capable of elucidating the laws and principles of interlearning and the various kinds of group learning visualized by proponents of lifelong education. Thus, the first area for further research requires the development of this broad area of applied psychological research.

Within the context of learning, much is made in writings about lifelong education of the transformation of the workplace, so that it becomes a place of education.  However, little is known of how this might be achieved.  Some expedients seem to have been tried such as the breakdown of the worker hierarchy and the development of self-management in Yugoslavia, but the sociology and psychology of the workplace have so far not developed clear answers concerning how it can be transformed so that it is capable of functioning in the ways envisaged by proponents of lifelong education, and spelled out at various points in the present volume.  Thus, an extended sociology and psychology of work are also called for.

Although it has been emphasized that evaluation of lifelong education should be qualitative as well as quantitative, it is not clear just what the relevant cost-benefit factors are. In particular, there is a need for clear specification of how lifelong education can be applied in developing countries, because they have both the greatest need for effective systems that can be rapidly developed, and also the best opportunity for making rapid and sweeping change, as they seek to throw off the effects of their colonial pasts.

Especially in the case of developed nations, it may be that it is a pipe dream to imagine that curricula as they currently exist will be scrapped wholesale, and replaced by new

ones based on the principles of lifelong education.  Some of
the reasons why such drastic change seems unlikely have already been discussed earlier in this chapter.  A more realistic
approach probably involves the view that certain elements of
existing curricula may possibly be strengthened and improved,
certain others eliminated or de-emphasized.  Thus, there is
pressing need for development of ways of analyzing existing curricula in order to identify the elements already in existence
which are most favourable to lifelong education, and to indicate how these elements could be given greater emphasis.

A major problem in fostering any curricular change is that
ideals or goals which find widespread acceptance as theory do
not survive long once they impinge upon the day-to-day activities of schools.  Thus, principles espoused enthusiastically at
teachers college or in in-service training courses are soon forgotten.  There is, therefore, need for research concerning how
to provide back up or support services which will help the
ideas of lifelong education survive in real life.  This might,
for example, involve short in-service courses, provision of
"trouble shooter" services in the form of visiting teachers,
banks of aids and materials, and many others.

In a similar vein, the school itself is an ongoing system
with a dynamism of its own.  This system contains both factors
hostile to the adoption or survival of lifelong education, and
also factors favourable to it.  An important practical question
is that of identifying the factors in existing school practices,
methods, philosophies and techniques which are favourable to
the survival of ideas deriving from the principles of lifelong
education, and those which are unfavourable.  These would be
expected to differ from country to country, one society stressing group learning methods or linking of work and school,
another emphasizing self-evaluation or the use of out-of-school
life educators, and so on.  Again, the aim would be to strength-
en and support positive elements.


*The prospects for lifelong education*

Whether the principles of lifelong education will actually
take firm hold in school-level education on a world-wide basis
remains to be seen.  Experience with other educational reforms
suggests that it will not, in the sense that massive, rapid reorganizations and re-orientations will not spring up, overnight,
as it were.  However, there will probably be a slow change of
emphasis and opinion in educational circles, with certain kinds
of activities coming to be more and more widely accepted.  As

Duke (1976) put it, proponents of lifelong education will probably have to be content to proceed by "stealth", rather than
taking the world by storm.  Some examples he gives of changes
predicted for the next 25 years (he was writing about Australia,
but his predictions look to have wider significance) include
the emergence of values emphasizing pluralism, diversity, democratization and improved quality of life, de-emphasis of
schools as the sole source of education, debureaucratization
of schooling, along with its democratization and diversifica-
tion, recognition of work and life experiences as important job
credentials, and the integration of school experiences with work
and the everyday life of the community.  Thus, provided that
they are content to proceed slowly, the prospects for advocates
of lifelong education look promising.

G

# References

Agoston, G. La communauté en tant qu'éducateur. *Acta Universitatis Szegedensis*, 1975, 18, 5-15.

Ainsworth, M.D. Reversible and irreversible effects of maternal deprivation on intellectual development. In O.J. Harvey (Ed.), *Experience structure and adaptability*. New York: Springer, 1966.

Anastasi, A. *Differential psychology*. New York: Macmillan, 1958 (3rd ed.).

Anastasi, A. Heredity, environment, and the question "How?". *Psychological Review*, 1958, 65, 197-208.

Anderson, H.H. The measurement of domination and of socially integrative behaviour in teachers' contacts with children. *Child Development*, 1939, 73-89.

Anderson, H.H., & Brewer, H.M. Studies of teachers' classroom personalities, I: Dominative and socially integrative behaviour of kindergarten teachers. *Applied psychology Monographs*, 1945, Whole No. 6.

Anderson, H.H., & Brewer, J.E. Studies of teachers' classroom personalities, II: Effects of teachers' dominative and integrative contacts on children's classroom behaviour. *Applied Psychology Monographs*, 1946, Whole No. 8.

Anderson, H.H., Brewer, J.E., & Reed, M.F. Studies of teachers' classroom personalities, III: Follow-up studies of the effects of dominative and integrative contacts on children's behaviour. *Applied psychology Monographs*, 1946, Whole No. 11.

Aron, R. *Progress and disillusion*. London: Pall Mall, 1968.

Asian Institute of Educational Administration and Planning, *Lifelong education*. (Report of the Meeting of Experts, New Delhi, August 1970). Delhi: Asian Institute of Educational Administration and Planning, 1970.

Aujaleu, E. Medicine of the future. *World Health*, 1973 (April), 23-29.

Bandura, A., & Walters, R.H. *Social learning and personality development*. New York: Holt, Rinehart and Winston, 1963.

Bartoshuk, A.K. Human neonatal cardiac responses to sound: a power function. *Psychonomic Science*, 1964, 1, 151-152.

Baumrind, D. Child care practices anteceding three patterns of preschool behaviour. *Genetic Psychology Monographs*, 1967, 75, 43-88.

Bayley, N. On the growth of intelligence. *American Psychologist*, 1955, 10, 805-818.

Bayley, N. Behavioural correlates of mental growth: birth to thirty-six years. *American Psychologist*, 1968, 23, 1-17.

Bayley, N., & Oden, M.H. The maintenance of intellectual ability in gifted adults. *Journal of Gerontology*, 1955, 10, 91-107.

Bengtsson, J. Recurrent education and manpower training. *Adult Training*, 1975, 2, 7-9.

Bennett, N. *Teaching styles and pupil progress*. London: Open Books, 1976.

Berg, I. *Education and jobs: The great training robbery*. New York: Praeger, 1970.

Berlyne, D.E. The influence of complexity and novelty in visual figures on orienting responses. *Journal of Experimental Psychology*, 1958, 55, 289-296.

Biggs, J.B. *Information and human learning*. Melbourne: Cassell, 1968.

Biggs, J.B. Content to process. *Australian Journal of Education*, 1973, 17, 225-238.

Bischoff, L.J.   *Adult psychology*.   New York: Harper and Row, 1969.

Blakely, R.J.   In Dumazedier, J. (with others)   *The school and continuing education*.   Paris: UNESCO, 1972.

Bloom, B.S. (Ed.), *Taxonomy of educational objectives*.   New York: Longmans Green, 1956.

Bloom, B.S.   *Stability and change in human characteristics*.   New York: Wiley, 1964.

Bloom, B.S.   *Human characteristics and school learning*.   New York: McGraw Hill, 1976.

Bowles, S.   Cuban education and the revolutionary ideology.   *Harvard Educational Review*, 1971, 41, 472-500.

Bradway, K.P., & Thompson, C.W.   Intelligence at adulthood: A twenty-five year follow-up.   *Journal of Educational Psychology*, 1962, 53, 1-14.

Brock, A.   Blueprint for a learning society.   *UNESCO Courier*, 1972, (November), 4-5.

Bromley, D.B.   *The psychology of human ageing*.   Harmondsworth, Middlesex: Penguin, 1974 (2nd ed.).

Brophy, J.E., & Good, T.L.   Teachers' communication of differential expectations for children's classroom performance: Some behavioural data.   *Journal of Educational Psychology*, 1970, 61, 365-374.

Bruner, J.S.   Going beyond the information given.   In J.S. Bruner et al., *Contemporary approaches to cognition*.   Cambridge, Mass.: Harvard University Press, 1957.

Bruner, J.S.   The course of cognitive growth.   *American Psychologist*, 1964, 19, 1-15.

Bruner, J.S.   *Processes of cognitive growth*: Infancy.   Barre, Mass.: Barre Publishers, 1968.

Bruner, J.S., & Olson, D.R.   Learning through experience and learning through media.   *Prospects: Quarterly Review of Education*, 1973, 3, 20-38.

Bruner, J.S., & Olver, R.R.  The development of equivalence transformations in children.  In J.C. Wright & J. Kagan (Eds.), Basic cognitive processes in children.  *Child Development Monographs*, 1963, 28, Whole No. 86.

Bühler, C.  The curve of life as studied in biographies.  *Journal of Applied Psychology*, 1935, 19, 405-409.

Bühler, C.  Genetic aspects of the self.  *Annals of New York Academy of Sciences*, 1962, 96, 730-764.

Burnett, A., Beach, H.D., & Sullivan, A.M.  Intelligence in a restricted environment.  *Canadian Psychologist*, 1963, 4, 126-136.

Burt, C.  The differentiation of intellectual ability.  *British Journal of Educational Psychology*, 1954, 24, 76-90.

Burt, C.  The genetic determination of differences in intelligence:  A study of monozygotic twins reared together and apart.  *British Journal of Psychology*, 1966, 57, 137-153.

Campbell, D.P.  A cross-sectional and longitudinal study of scholastic abilities over twenty-five years.  *Journal of Counselling Psychology*, 1965, 12, 55-61.

Canastrari, R.E.  Paced and self-paced learning in young and elderly adults.  *Journal of Gerontology*, 1963, 18, 165-168.

Chow, K.L., Riesen, A.H., & Newell, F.W.  Degeneration of retinal ganglion cells in infant chimpanzees reared in darkness.  *Journal of Comparative Neurology*, 1957, 107, 27-42.

Cirtautas, K.  *The refugee:  A psychological study*.  Boston: Meador Publishing Co., 1957.

Coleman, J.S. (with others)  *Equality of educational opportunity*.  Washington, D.C.: U.S. Government Printing Office, 1966.

Coleman, J.S.  How do the young become adults?  *Review of Educational Research*, 1972, 42, 431-439.

Coles, E.K.T.  Universities and adult education.  *International Review of Education*, 1972, 18, 172-182.

Comfort, A.  *Ageing: The biology of senescence*.  London:

Routledge and Kegan Paul, 1964 (2nd ed.).

Comfort, A. The prolongation of vigorous life. *Impact of Science on Society*, 1970, 20, 307-319.

Corsini, R.J., & Fassett, K.K. Intelligence and aging. *Journal of Genetic Psychology*, 1953, 83, 249-264.

Coste, P. Is learning optimal in childhood? *Prospects: Quarterly Review of Education*, 1973, 3, 46-48.

Council of Europe, Notes of the Council of Europe on permanent education. *Convergence*, *1968*. 1 (14), 50-53.

Covington, M.V. Productive thinking and a cognitive curriculum. Invited paper presented at the symposium *Studies of the inquiry process, problems of theory, description and teaching*. American Psychological Association Convention, Washington, D.C., 1967.

Cronbach, L.J. Year-to-year correlations of mental tests: A review of the Hofstaetter analysis. *Child Development*, 1967, 38, 283-289.

Cropley, A.J. Differentiation of abilities, socio-economic status and the WISC. *Journal of Consulting Psychology*, 1964, 28, 512-517.

Cropley, A.J. Lifelong education: A panacea for all educational ills? *Australian Journal of Education*, 1974, 18, 1-15.

Cropley, A.J., & Gross, P.F. The effectiveness of computer-assisted instruction. *Alberta Journal of Educational Research*, 1970, 16, 203-210.

Cropley, A.J., & Sikand, J.S. Creativity and schizophrenia. *Journal of Consulting and Clinical Psychology*, 1973, 40, 462-468.

Dauber, H., Fritsch, H., Liegle, L., Sachs, W., Scheilke, C.T., & Spiekermann, M. Lebenslanges Lernen -- lebenslängliche Schule? Analyse und Kritik des OECD-Berichts "Recurrent Education". *Zeitschrift für Pädagogik*, 1975, 21, 173-192.

Dave, R.H. Lifelong education and school curriculum. *UNESCO Institute Monographs*, 1973, Whole No. 1.

Dave, R.H. (Ed.), *Foundations of lifelong education.* Oxford: Pergamon, 1976.

De'Ath, C. Anthropological and ecological foundations of lifelong education. In R.H. Dave (Ed.), *Foundations of lifelong education.* Oxford: Pergamon, 1976.

Delker, P.V. Governmental roles in lifelong education. *Journal of Research and Development in Education,* 1974, 7, 24-34.

Dennis, W. Causes of retardation among institutional children: Iran. *Journal of Genetic Psychology,* 1960, 96, 47-59.

Dennis, W. Creative productivity between the ages of 20 and 80 years. In B.L. Neugarten (Ed.), *Middle age and aging.* Chicago: University of Chicago Press, 1968.

Dewey, J. *Democracy and education.* New York: MacMillan, 1916.

Dockrell, W.B. Education, social class and development of ability. Unpublished doctoral dissertation, University of Chicago, 1963.

Dubin, S.S. The psychology of lifelong learning. New developments in the professions. *International Review of Applied Psychology,* 1974, 23, 17-31.

Dugdale, R.L. *"The Jukes" a study in crime, pauperism, disease and heredity, also further studies of criminals.* New York: Putnam, 1877.

Duke, C. *Australian perspectives in lifelong education.* Melbourne: Australian Council for Educational Research, 1976.

Dumazedier, J. (with others) *The school and continuing education.* Paris: UNESCO, 1972.

Durkheim, E. *Sociologie de l'éducation.* Paris: Presses Universitaires de France, 1961.

Educational Policies Commission, *Universal opportunity for early childhood education.* Washington, D.C.: National Education Association of the United States, 1966.

Eisdorfer, C. Arousal and performance: Experiments in verbal learning and a tentative theory. In G.A. Talland (Ed.),

*Human aging and behaviour*.  New York: Academic Press, 1968.

Eggleston, S.J.  Pre-school education in Europe.  *Paedagogica Europaea*, 1974, 9, 10-16.

Elvin, L.  Learning to be and world trends in education.  *Education News*, 1975, 15, 24-29.

Erikson, E.H.  Identity and the life cycle.  *Psychological Issues*, 1959, 1, 1-165.

Erikson, E.H.  *Identity, youth and crisis*.  New York: Norton, 1968.

Fantz, R.L.  Pattern vision in newborn infants.  *Science*, 1963, 140, 296-297.

Farmer, J.A.  Impact of "lifelong learning" on the professionalization of adult education.  *Journal of Research and Development in Education*, 1974, 7, 57-65.

Faure E. (with others)  *Learning to be: The world of education today and tomorrow*.  Paris and London: UNESCO and Harrap, 1972.

Ferguson, G.A.  On learning and human ability.  *Canadian Journal of Psychology*, 1954, 8, 95-112.

Fischer, C.  Intelligence defined as effectiveness of approaches.  *Journal of Consulting and Clinical Psychology*, 1969, 33, 668-674.

Flavell, J.H.  *The developmental psychology of Jean Piaget*.  New York: Van Nostrand, 1963.

Foulds, G.A., & Raven, J.C.  Normal changes in the mental abilities of adults as age advances.  *Journal of Mental Science*, 1948, 94, 133-142.

Fox, C., & Birren, J.E.  The differential decline of subtest scores of the Wechsler-Bellevue Intelligence Scale in 60-69-year old individuals.  *Journal of Genetic Psychology*, 1950, 77, 313-317.

Freeberg, N.E., & Payne, D.T.  Parental influence on cognitive development in early childhood: A review.  *Child Development*,

1967, 38, 65-87

Frese, H.H. Permanent education -- dream or nightmare? *Education and Culture*, 1972, 19, 9-13.

Friedmann, E.A., & Havighurst, R.J. *The meaning of work and retirement*. Chicago: University of Chicago Press, 1954.

Friend, C.M., & Zubek, J.P. The effect of age on critical thinking ability. *Journal of Gerontology*, 1958, 13, 407-413.

Galton, F. *Hereditary genius: An inquiry into its laws and consequences*. London: Macmillan, 1869.

Galton, F. *Inquiries into human faculty and its development*. New York: Macmillan, 1883.

Garrett, H.E. A developmental theory of intelligence. *American Psychologist*, 1946, 1, 372-378.

Gelpi, E. Education permanente et troisième âge dans les sociétés industrialisées. *Paideia*, 1976, 6, 189-192.

Gintis, H. Education, technology and the characteristics of worker productivity. *American Economic Review*, 1971, 61, 2, 266-279.

Goddard, H.H. *The Kallikak Family: a study in the heredity of feeblemindedness*. New York: Macmillan, 1912.

Gordon, H. *Mental and scholastic tests among retarded children*. Education Pamphlet No. 44. London: Her Majesty's Printer, 1923.

Gottesman, I.I. Heritability of personality: a demonstration. *Psychological Monographs*, 1963, 77, Whole No. 572.

Goulet, L.R., & Baltes, P.B. (Eds.), *Lifespan developmental psychology*. New York: Academic Press, 1970.

Granick, S. Morale measures as related to personality, cognitive and medical functioning of the aged. *Proceedings of the 81st Annual Convention of the American Psychological Association*, Montreal, Canada. 1973, 8, 785-786.

Gray, J., & Satterley, D.  A chapter of errors: "Teaching Styles and Pupils Progress" in retrospect. *Educational Research*, 1976, 19, 45-56.

Green, R.F.  Age-intelligence relationships between ages sixteen and sixty-four: A rising trend. *Developmental Psychology*, 1969, 1, 618-627.

Greenberg, D.J., Uzgaris, I.C., & Hunt, J.M.  Hastening the development of the blink-response with looking. *Journal of Genetic Psychology*, 1968, 113, 167-176.

Harlow, H.F.  The development of affectional patterns in infant monkeys. In B.M. Foss (Ed.), *Determinants of infant behaviour*. Vol. 1. London: Methuen, 1961.

Havighurst, R.J.  *Human development and education*.  New York: Longmans Green, 1953.

Havighurst, R.J.  Adulthood and old age.  In R.L. Ebel (Ed.), *Encyclopedia of educational research*.  New York: Macmillan, 1969.

Hebb, D.O.  *The organization of behaviour*.  New York: Wiley, 1949.

Hess, R.D., & Shipman, V.  Early experience and the socialization of cognitive modes in children.  *Child Development*, 1965, 36, 869-886.

Hicter, M.  Education for a changing world.  *Prospects: Quarterly Review of Education*, 1972, 2, 298-312.

Hiemstra, R.  Community adult education in lifelong learning.  *Journal of Research and Development in Education*, 1974, 7, 34-43.

Hinzen, H., & Hundsdörfer, V.H. (Eds.)  Education for liberation and development.  The Tanzanian approach towards lifelong education.  *Experiments and Innovations in Education*, 1977 (in press).

Hirt, M.L.  Aptitude changes as a function of age.  *Personnel and Guidance Journal*, 1964, 43, 174-176.

Hofstaetter, P.R.  The changing composition of "intelligence": a study in T-technique.  *Journal of Genetic Psychology*, 1954, 85, 159-162.

Horn, J.L.  Organization of abilities and the development of intelligence.  *Psychological Review*, 1968, 75, 242-259.

Horn, J.L., & Donaldson, G.  On the myth of intellectual decline in adulthood.  *American Psychologist*, 1976, 31, 701-719.

Houle, C.O., & Houle, B.  The continuity of life.  In Asian Institute of Educational Administration and Planning, *Lifelong education*.  (Report of the Meeting of Experts, New Delhi, August 1970).  Delhi: Asian Institute of Educational Administration and Planning, 1970.

Hudson, W.  Pictorial depth perception in sub-culture groups in Africa.  *Journal of Social Psychology*, 1960, 52, 183-208.

Hunt, J. McV.  *Intelligence and experience*.  New York: Ronald, 1961.

Hunt, J. McV.  Heredity, environment, and class or ethnic differences.  In *Assessment in a pluralistic society*.  Proceedings of the 1972 Invitational Conference on Testing Problems.  Princeton: ETS, 1973.

Hutt, S.J.  Biological aspects of early development.  *Paedagogica Europaea*, 1974, 9, 18-31.

IBE, Final Report of the International Conference on Education, 35th Session, Geneva, August 27 - September 4, 1975.  Geneva: IBE, 1975.

Illich, I., & Verne, E.  Le piège de l'école à vie.  *Le Monde de l'Education*, 1975 (January), 11-14.

Inhelder, B., & Piaget, J.  *The growth of intelligence from early childhood to adolescence*.  New York: Basic Books, 1958.

Jacks, M.L.  *Total education; a plea for synthesis*.  London: Paul, Trench, Trubner, 1946.

James, W. *The principles of psychology*. New York: Holt, 1890.

Jansen, M., Jensen, P.E., & Mylov, P. Teacher characteristics and other factors affecting classroom interaction and teacher behaviour. *International Review of Education*, 1972, 18, 529-540.

Jencks, C. (with others) *Inequality: A reassessment of the effect of family and schooling in America*. New York: Basic Books, 1972.

Jerome, E.A. Decay of heuristic processes in the aged. In C. Tibbitts and W. Donahue (Eds.), *Aging around the world*. Proceedings of the Fifth Congress of the International Association of Gerontology. New York: Columbia University Press, 1962.

Johnson, L. Mathew Arnold's concept of culture and its significance for R.S. Peters' analysis of education. *Australian Journal of Education*, 1972, 16, 165-174.

Johnstone, J.W.C., & Rivera, R.J. *Volunteers for learning: A study of the educational pursuits of American adults*. Chicago: Aldine, 1965.

Jones, H.E., & Conrad, H.W. The growth and decline of intelligence. *Genetic Psychology Monographs*, 1933, 13, 223-298.

Kagan, J. Acquisition and significance of sex-typing and sex role identity. In M.L. Hoffman and L.W. Hoffman (Eds.), *Review of child development research*, Vol. I. New York: Sage, 1964.

Kagan, J., & Moss, H.A. Stability and validity of achievement fantasy. *Journal of Abnormal and Social Psychology*, 1959, 58, 357-364.

Kagan, J., Henker, B.A., Hen-Tov, A., Levine, J., & Lewis, M. Infants' differential reactions to familiar and distorted faces. *Child Development*, 1966, 37, 519-532.

Kessen, W. Sucking and looking two organized congenital patterns of behaviour in the human newborn. In H.W. Stevenson, E.H. Hess & H.L. Rheingold (Eds.), *Early behaviour: Comparative and developmental approaches*. New York: Wiley, 1967.

Kidd, J.R.  The Third International Conference: Tokyo.
  *Convergence*, 1972, 5 (3), 15-19.

Kinsey, A.C., Pomeroy, W.B., & Martin, C.E.  *Sexual behaviour
  in the human male.*  Philadelphia: Saunders, 1948.

Klein, G.S.  The personal world through perception.  In R.R.
  Blake & G.V. Ramsey (Eds.), *Perception: An approach to personality.*  New York: Ronald, 1951.

Klein, G.S.  *Perception, motives, and personality.*  New York:
  Knopf, 1970.

Knowles, M.S.  Non-traditional study -- Issues and resolutions.
  *Adult Leadership*, 1975, 23, 232-235.

Knox, A.B.  Clientele analysis.  *Review of Educational Research*,
  1965, 35, 231-239.

Koestler, A.  *The act of creation.*  London: Hutchinson, 1964.

Kovacs, M.L., & Cropley, A.J.  Alienation and the assimilation
  of immigrants.  *Australian Journal of Social Issues*, 1975,
  10, 221-229.

Kuhlen, R.G.  Motivational changes during the adult years.  In
  R.G. Kuhlen (Ed.), *Psychological backgrounds of adult educa-
  tion.*  Chicago: Centre for the Study of Liberal Education for
  Adults, 1963.

Kupisiewicz, C.  On some principles of modernizing the school
  system as a base for adult education.  *Convergence*, 1972, 5
  (3), 15-19.

Kyöstiö, O.K.  The changing role of school in society.  *International Review of Education*, 1972, 18, 339-351.

Kyrasek, J., & Polisensky, J.V.  Comenius and all-embracing
  education.  *Convergence*, 1968, 1 (4), 80-86.

Lally, J.R.  Infancy to three years of age.  In Dumazedier, J.
  (with others) *The school and continuing education.*  Paris:
  UNESCO, 1972.

Lehman, H.C.  *Age and achievement.*  Princeton University Press,
  1953.

Lengrand, P. *An introduction to lifelong education*. Paris: UNESCO, 1970.

Leventhal, A.S., & Lipsitt, L.P. Adaptation, pitch discrimination, and sound localization in the neonate. *Child Development*, 1964, 35, 759-767.

Lindeman, E.C. *The meaning of adult education*. Montreal: Harvest House, 1961.

Lipsitt, L.P. Learning in the human infant. In H.W. Stevenson, R. Hess, & H.L. Rheingold (Eds.), *Early behaviour: Comparative and developmental approaches*. New York: Wiley, 1967.

Livingstone, R.W. *Education for a world adrift*. Cambridge: Cambridge University Press, 1943.

London, J. *Adult education outlines as an emerging field of university study*. Chicago: University of Chicago Press, 1964.

Lorge, I. The influence of the test upon the nature of mental decline as a function of age. *Journal of Educational Psychology*, 1936, 27, 100-110.

Luria, A.R. *The role of speech in the regulation of normal and abnormal behaviour*. London: Pergamon, 1961.

Lynch, J., & Plunkett, H.D. *Teacher education and cultural change*. London: Allen & Unwin, 1973.

Margulies, N., & Raia, A.P. Scientists, engineers and technological obsolescence. *California Management Review*, 1967, 10, 43-48.

McDavid, J.W., & Harari, H. *Social psychology*. New York: Harper & Row, 1968.

McFarland, R., & O'Doherty, B. Work and occupational skills. In J.E. Birren (Ed.), *Handbook of aging and the individual*. Chicago: University of Chicago Press, 1959.

McLeish, J. *The science of behaviour*. London: Barrie & Rockcliff, 1963.

Menyuk, P. *The acquisition and development of language*. Englewood Cliffs, New Jersey: Prentice Hall, 1971.

Miles, V.C., & Miles, W.R.  The correlation of intelligence
scores and chronological age from early to late maturity.
*American Journal of Psychology*, 1932, 44-78.

Ministry of Reconstruction Adult Education Committee, *Report of
the Ministry of Reconstruction Adult Education Committee*.
London: H.M.'s Stationery Office, 1919.

Musgrave, P.W.  Changing society: some underlying assumptions
of the Karmel Report.  *Australian Journal of Education*, 1975,
19, 1-14.

Naylor, G.F.K., & Harwood, E.  Mental exercises for grandmother.
*Education News*, 1970, 12 (11), 15-18.

Neugarten, B.L. (Ed.), *Middle age and aging*.  Chicago: University of Chicago Press, 1968.

Nisbet, J.D.  Contributions to intelligence testing and the
theory of intelligence: IV. Intelligence and age: Retesting
with twenty-four years' interval.  *British Journal of Educational Psychology*, 1957, 27, 190-198.

Ohliger, J.  Is lifelong adult education a guarantee of permanent inadequacy?  *Convergence*, 1974, 7 (2), 47-59.

Olford, J.E.  Deschooling further education.  *The New Era*, 1972,
53, 202-204.

Owens, W.A.  Age and mental abilities: a longitudinal study.
*Genetic Psychology Monographs*, 1953, 48, 3-54.

Owens, W.A., & Charles, D.C.  *Life history correlates of age
changes in mental abilities*.  Lafayette, Indiana: Purdue
University Press, 1963.

Parkyn, G.W.  *Towards a conceptual model of lifelong education*.
UNESCO Educational Studies and Documents, Number 12.  Paris:
UNESCO, 1973.

Paul, I.H.  Studies in remembering.  *Psychological Issues*,
Monograph No. 2, New York: International Universities Press,
1959.

Peck, R.  Psychological development in the second half of life.
In J.E. Anderson (Ed.), *Psychological aspects of aging*.

Washington, D.C.: American Psychological Association, 1956.

Phillips, J.L. *The origins of intellect:  Piaget's theory.* San Francisco: Freeman, 1969.

Plowden Report. *Children and their primary schools,* Report of the Central Advisory Council for Education (England). London: H.M.'s Stationery Office, 1967.

Pressey, S.L.  Potentials of age: an exploratory field study. *Genetic Psychology Monographs,* 1951, 56, 159-205.

Pressey, S.L., & Kuhlen, R.G. *Psychological development through the life span.* New York: Harper, 1957.

Richmond, W.K.  Lifelong education. *British Book News,* 1973 (July), 420-427.

Rohwer, W.D.  Cognitive development and education. In P.H. Mussen (Ed.), *Carmichael's manual of child psychology.* New York: Wiley, 1970 (3rd ed.).

Rohwer, W.D.  Prime time for education: Early childhood or adolescence? *Harvard Educational Review,* 1971, 41, 316-341.

Röman, K.  A review of pre-school experiments and research in Finland. *Paedagogica Europaea,* 1974, 9, 163-171.

Sarbin, T.R.  Notes on the transformation of social identity. In L.M. Roberts, N.S. Greenfield & M.H. Miller (Eds.), *Comprehensive mental health: The challenge of evaluation.* Madison, Wisconsin: University of Wisconsin Press, 1968.

Sayegh, Y., & Dennis, W.  The effects of supplementary experiences upon the behavioural development of infants in institutions. *Child Development,* 1965, 36, 81-90.

Schaeffer, H.R.  The development of social attachments in infancy. *Child Development Monographs,* 1964, 29, Whole No. 94.

Schaie, K.W.  A reinterpretation of age-related changes in cognitive structure and functioning.  In L.R. Goulet & P.B. Baltes (Eds.), *Lifespan developmental psychology: Research and theory.* New York: Academic Press, 1970.

Schaie, K.W.  Translations in gerontology - From lab to life.

Intellectual functioning. *American Psychologist*, 1974, 29, 802-807.

Schaie, K.W., & Labouvie-Vief, G. Generational versus ento-genetic components of change in adult cognitive behaviour: A fourteen-year consequential study. *Developmental Psychology*, 1974, 10, 105-120.

Schonfield, D. Translations in gerontology - From lab to life. Utilizing information. *American Psychologist*, 1974, 29, 796-801.

Schroder, H.M., Driver, M.J., & Streufert, S. *Human information processing*. New York: Holt, Rinehart & Winston, 1967.

Schubert, J., & Cropley, A.J. Verbal regulation of behaviour and IQ in Canadian Indian and White children. *Developmental Psychology*, 1972, 7, 295-301.

Scott, J.P. *Aggression*. Chicago: University of Chicago Press, 1958.

Selowsky, M. *The effects of unemployment and growth on the rate of return to education: The case of Colombia*. (Economic Development Report No. 116). Cambridge, Mass.: Harvard University Center for International Affairs, 1968.

Silva, A. Education for freedom. *Prospects: Quarterly Review of Education*, 1973, 3, 39-45.

Simmons, J. The report of the Faure Commission: One step forward and two steps back. *Higher Education*, 1973, 2, 475-488.

Simmons, J., & Erkut, S. *Schooling for development? Students and workers in Tunisia*. Cambridge, Mass.: Harvard University Press, 1972.

Skager, R., & Dave, R.H. *Developing criteria and procedures for the evaluation of school curriculum in the perspective of lifelong education*. Oxford: Pergamon, 1977.

Skeels, H.M., & Dye, H.B. A study of the effects of differential stimulation of mentally retarded children. *Preceedings of the American Association on Mental Deficiency*, 1939, 44, 114-136.

Smart, R.C.   The changing composition of "intelligence": A Replication of a factor analysis. *Journal of Genetic Psychology*, 1965, 107, 111-116.

Soar, R.   Teacher behaviour related to pupil growth. *International Review of Education*, 1972, 18, 508-528.

Sontag, L.W., Baker, C.T., & Nelson, V.   Mental growth and personality: a longitudinal study. *Child Development Monographs*, 1958, 23, Whole No. 68.

Stephens, J.M.   *The process of schooling: A psychological examination*. New York: Holt, Rinehart & Winston, 1967.

Stone, L.J., Murphy, L.B., & Smith, H.T. (Eds.), *The competent infant: Research and comment*. New York: Basic Books, 1972.

Suchodolski, B.   Out of school. *Prospects: Quarterly Review of Education*, 1972, 2, 142-154.

Suchodolski, B.   Education between being and having. *Prospects: Quarterly Journal of Education*, 1976, 6, 163-180.

Sward, K.   Age and mental ability in superior men. *American Journal of Psychology*, 1945, 58, 443-479.

Swedish Ministry of Education,   Motives for recurrent education. *Convergence*, 1972, 5 (4), 54-62.

Terrell, G., Durkin, K., & Wiesley, M.   Social class and the nature of the incentive in discrimination learning. *Journal of Abnormal and Social Psychology*, 1959, 59, 270-272.

Tough, A.   *The adult's learning projects*. Toronto: OISE, 1971.

Tuddenham, R.D.   Soldier intelligence in World Wars I and II. *American Psychologist*, 1948, 3, 54-56.

Tyler, L.E.   *The psychology of human differences*. New York: Appleton-Century-Crofts, 1965 (3rd ed.).

UNESCO,   Working paper on the contribution of persons other than teachers to educational activities in the perspective of lifelong education. UNESCO Symposium, Paris 13-17 September, 1976,

Vernon, P.E. *The structure of human abilities*. London: Methuen, 1950.

Vernon, P.E. *Intelligence and cultural environment*. London: Methuen, 1969.

Vincent, D.F. The linear relationship between age and score of adults in intelligence tests. *Occupational Psychology*, 1952, 26, 243-249.

Vinokur, A. Economic analysis of lifelong education. In R.H. Dave (Ed.), *Foundations of lifelong education*. Oxford: Pergamon, 1976.

Von Senden, M. *Space and sight*. (Translated by P. Heath) London: Methuen, 1960.

Vygotsky, L.S. *Thought and language*. New York: Wiley, 1962.

Walk, R.D., & Gibson, E.J. A comparative study of visual depth perception. *Psychological Monographs*, 1961, 75, Whole No. 519.

Ward, C. Anarchy and education. *The New Era*, 1972, 53, 179-184.

Weaver, A. Conviviality and "learning webs". *The New Era*, 1972, 53, 171-173.

Wechsler, D. *The measurement and appraisal of adult intelligence*. Baltimore: Williams and Wilkins, 1958 (4th ed.).

Welford, A.T. Age and skill: Motor, intellectual and social. *Interdisciplinary Topics in Gerontology*, 1969, 4, 1-22.

Wheeler, L.R. A comparative study of the intelligence of East Tennessee mountain children. *Journal of Educational Psychology*, 1942, 33, 321-334.

Witken, H.A. Origins of cognitive style. In C. Scheerer (Ed.), *Cognition: Theory, research, promise*. New York: Harper and Row, 1964.

Worth, W.H. (with others) *A choice of futures*. Edmonton: Queen's Printer for the Province of Alberta, 1972.

Yerkes, R.M. (Ed.), *Psychological examining in the U.S. Army.*
  Memoirs of National Academy of Science, Vol. 15, 1921.

Zhamin, V.A., & Kostanian, S.L.   Education and Soviet Economic
  growth.  *International Review of Education*, 1972, 18, 155-170.

# Index

185

Baumrind, D., 30, 167
Bayley, N., 54, 71, 167
Beach, H.D., 72, 169
Bengtsson, J., 20, 29, 167
Bennett, N., 46, 47, 167
Berg, I., 114, 167
Berlyne, D.E., 72, 167
Biggs, J.B., 96, 124, 137, 138, 167
Birren, J.E., 57, 172
Binet, A., 54
Bischoff, L.J., 73, 168
Blakely, R.J., 34, 36, 39, 168
Bloom, B.S., 30, 32, 69, 70,
  106, 168
Bowles, S., 21, 23, 108, 160,
  168
Bradway, K.P., 64, 168
Brewer, H.M., 115, 166
Brock, A., 130, 168
Bromley, D.B., 67, 73, 74, 168
Brophy, J.E., 115, 168
Bruner, J.S., 21, 30, 71, 91,
  92, 106, 121, 124, 168, 169
Bühler, C., 97, 98, 169
Burnett, A., 72, 169
Burt, C., 82, 105, 169


Campbell, D.P., 64, 169
Canastrari, R.E., 60, 169
Cattell, R.B., 59
Change
  alienation and, 13, 110, 131
  challenge of, 12, 128
  coping with, 12-13, 130, 132,
    137, 138, 159
  education and, 16, 22, 125,
    130, 132, 137, 161
  psychological effects of,
    13, 110, 130
  social, 12-13, 131, 159
  specialization and effects
    of, 76, 129
  technology and, 12-13, 161
  values and, 25, 110, 130
  work and, 12-13, 27

Childhood
  basis of later development,
    14, 19, 30, 68, 69, 71,
    124
  cognition in, 70ff, 86, 94
  competence in, 29, 71
  curriculum for early,
    124-126
  development in, 30, 70ff,
    71, 72, 94, 120
  education and, 14-15, 29,
    30, 101, 150
  environment and develop-
    ment in, 69, 124
  learning during, 30, 31,
    32, 53, 56, 78, 101, 119
  lifelong education and,
    29, 124-126
  plasticity in, 120
  socialization and, 26,
    100-101, 106
Charles, D.C., 64, 179
Cheydleur, F.D., 75
Chow, K.L., 71, 169
Cirtautas, K., 109, 169
Cognition
  abstract thinking and, 71,
    72, 87-88, 89, 90, 94
  childhood and, 71, 72, 124
  classroom implications of,
    94
  coding in, 79-80, 84, 91
  cognitive curriculum, 131
  cognitive styles, 84-85,
    121
  definition of, 79-81
  development of, 70, 79ff,
    86, 87-88, 88-91, 93,
    106, 121
  early stimulation and, 15,
    86
  education and, 13, 31, 41,
    85, 114, 132
  individual differences in,
    84-85, 88, 91, 94, 121
  information and, 79-80, 84

Work (cont.)
  obsolescence and, 76
  productivity and lifelong
    education, 155
  psychological factors in,
    14, 107, 155, 160, 163
  qualifications of workers,
    20, 29
  roles at, 13, 25-27, 107,
    160

  workers as teachers, 108,
    134-135
Worth, W.H., 27, 30, 124, 125,
  183

Yerkes, R.M., 55, 96, 183

Zhamin, V.A., 24, 31, 184
Zubek, J.P., 59, 173